Romeo and Juliet

WILLIAM SHAKESPEARE

ROMEO

AND

JULIET

Introduction by William Hazlitt

THE MODERN LIBRARY

NEW YORK

2001 Modern Library Edition

LIBRARY OF CONGRESS CATALOGING-IN-PUBLICATION DATA
Shakespeare, William, 1564–1616.
Romeo and Juliet / William Shakespeare ; introduction by William Hazlitt.
p.   cm.
ISBN 0-679-64220-X
1. Verona (Italy)—Drama.   2. Vendetta—Drama.   3. Youth—Drama.   I. Title.
PR2831 .A1   2001
822.3'3—dc21   2001025336

Modern Library website address: www.modernlibrary.com

Printed in the United States of America on acid-free paper

2 4 6 8 9 7 5 3 1

CONTENTS

INTRODUCTION

William Hazlitt

Romeo and Juliet is the only tragedy which Shakespear has written entirely on a love-story. It is supposed to have been his first play,* and it deserves to stand in that proud rank. There is the buoyant spirit of youth in every line, in the rapturous intoxication of hope, and in the bitterness of despair. It has been said of *Romeo and Juliet* by a great critic, that "whatever is most intoxicating in the odour of a southern spring, languishing in the song of the nightingale, or voluptuous in the first opening of the rose, is to be found in this poem." The description is true; and yet it does not answer to our idea of the play. For if it has the sweetness of the rose, it has its freshness too; if it has the languor of the nightingale's song, it has also its giddy transport; if it has the softness of a southern spring, it is as glowing and as bright. There is nothing of a sickly and sentimental cast. Romeo and Juliet are in love, but they are not love-sick. Every thing speaks the very soul of pleasure, the high and healthy pulse of the passions: the heart beats, the blood circulates and mantles throughout. Their courtship is not an insipid interchange of sentiments lip-deep, learnt at second-hand from poems and plays,—made up of beauties of the most shadowy kind, of "fancies wan that hang the pensive head," of evanescent smiles, and sighs that breathe not, of delicacy that shrinks from the touch, and feebleness that scarce supports itself, an elaborate vacuity of thought,

---

*Editor's note: In fact, *Romeo and Juliet* was written between 1594 and 1596, a period when Shakespeare also produced *A Midsummer Night's Dream*, *The Merchant of Venice*, and *Richard II.*

and an artificial dearth of sense, spirit, truth, and nature! It is the reverse of all this. It is Shakespear all over, and Shakespear when he was young.

We have heard it objected to *Romeo and Juliet,* that it is founded on an idle passion between a boy and a girl, who have scarcely seen and can have but little sympathy or rational esteem for one another, who have had no experience of the good or ills of life, and whose raptures or despair must be therefore equally groundless and fantastical. Whoever objects to the youth of the parties in this play as "too unripe and crude" to pluck the sweets of love, and wishes to see a first-love carried on into a good old age, and the passions taken at the rebound, when their force is spent, may find all this done in the *Stranger* and in other German plays, where they do things by contraries, and transpose nature to inspire sentiment and create philosophy. Shakespear proceeded in a more strait-forward, and, we think, effectual way. He did not endeavour to extract beauty from wrinkles, or the wild throb of passion from the last expiring sigh of indifference. He did not "gather grapes of thorns nor figs of thistles." It was not his way. But he has given a picture of human life, such as it is in the order of nature. He has founded the passion of the two lovers not on the pleasures they had experienced, but on all the pleasures they had *not* experienced. All that was to come of life was theirs. At that untried source of promised happiness they slaked their thirst, and the first eager draught made them drunk with love and joy. They were in full possession of their senses and their affections. Their hopes were of air, their desires of fire. Youth is the season of love, because the heart is then first melted in tenderness from the touch of novelty, and kindled to rapture, for it knows no end of its enjoyments of its wishes. Desire has no limit but itself. Passion, the love and expectation of pleasure, is infinite, extravagant, inexhaustible, till experience comes to check and kill it. Juliet exclaims on her first interview with Romeo—

> "My bounty is as boundless as the sea,
> My love as deep."

And why should it not? What was to hinder the thrilling tide of pleasure, which had just gushed from her heart, from flowing on without stint or measure, but experience which she was yet without? What was to abate the transport of the first sweet sense of pleasure, which her heart and her senses had just tasted, but indifference which she was yet a stranger to? What was there to check the ardour of hope, of faith, of constancy, just rising in her breast, but disappointment which she had not yet felt! As are the desires and the hopes of youthful passion, such is the keenness of its disappointments, and their baleful effect. Such is the transition in this play from the highest bliss to the lowest despair, from the nuptial couch to an untimely grave. The only evil that even in apprehension befalls the two lovers is the loss of the greatest possible felicity; yet this loss is fatal to both, for they had rather part with life than bear the thought of surviving all that had made life dear to them. In all this, Shakespear has but followed nature, which existed in his time, as well as now. The modern philosophy, which reduces the whole theory of the mind to habitual impressions, and leaves the natural impulses of passion and imagination out of the account, had not then been discovered; or if it had, would have been little calculated for the uses of poetry.

It is the inadequacy of the same false system of philosophy to account for the strength of our earliest attachments, which has led Mr. Wordsworth to indulge in the mystical visions of Platonism in his Ode on the Progress of Life. He has very admirably described the vividness of our impressions in youth and childhood, and how "they fade by degrees into the light of common day," and he ascribes the change to the supposition of a pre-existent state, as if our early thoughts were nearer heaven, reflections of former trails of glory, shadows of our past being. This is idle. It is not from the knowledge of the past that the first impressions of things derive their gloss and splendour, but from our ignorance of the future, which fills the void to come with the warmth of our desires, with our gayest hopes, and brightest fancies. It is the obscurity spread before it that colours the prospect of life with hope, as it is the cloud which reflects the rainbow. There is no occasion to resort to any mystical union and transmission of feeling through different states of being to account for the romantic enthusiasm of youth; nor to plant the root of hope in the grave, nor to derive it from the skies. Its root is in the heart of man: it lifts its head above the stars. Desire and imagination are inmates of the human breast. The heaven "that lies about us in our infancy" is only a new world, of which we know nothing but what we wish it to be, and believe all that we wish. In youth and boyhood, the world we live in is the world of desire, and of fancy: it is experience that brings us down to the world of reality. What is it that in youth sheds a dewy light round the evening star? That makes the daisy look so bright? That perfumes the hyacinth? That embalms the first kiss of love? It is the delight of novelty, and the seeing no end to the pleasure that we fondly believe is still in store for us. The heart revels in the luxury of its own thoughts, and is unable to sustain the weight of hope and love that presses upon it.—The effects of the passion of love alone might have dissipated Mr. Wordsworth's theory, if he means any thing more by it than an ingenious and poetical allegory. *That* at least is not a link in the chain let down from other worlds; "the purple light of love" is not a dim reflection of the smiles of celestial bliss. It does not appear till the middle of life, and then seems like "another morn risen on mid-day." In this respect the soul comes into the world "in utter nakedness." Love waits for the ripening of the youthful blood. The sense of pleasure precedes the love of pleasure, but with the sense of pleasure, as soon as it is felt, come thronging infinite desires and hopes of pleasure, and love is mature as soon as born. It withers and it dies almost as soon!

This play presents a beautiful *coup-d'ail* of the progress of human life. In thought it occupies years, and embraces the circle of the affections from childhood to old age. Juliet has become a great girl, a young woman since we first remember her a little thing in the idle prattle of the nurse. Lady Capulet was about her age when she became a mother, and old Capulet somewhat impatiently tells his younger visitors,

> —— "I have seen the day
> That I have worn a visor, and could tell
> A whispering tale in a fair lady's ear
> Such as would please; 'tis gone, 'tis gone, 'tis gone."

Thus one period of life makes way for the following, and one generation pushes another off the stage. One of the most striking passages to show the intense feeling of youth in this play is Capulet's invitation to Paris to visit his entertainment.

> "At my poor house look to behold this night
> Earth-treading stars that make dark heaven light:
> Such comfort as do lusty young men feel
> When well-apparell'd April on the heel
> Of limping winter treads, even such delight
> Among fresh female buds shall you this night
> Inherit at my house."

The feelings of youth and of the spring are here blended together like the breath of opening flowers. Images of vernal beauty appear to have floated before the author's mind, in writing this poem, in profusion. Here is another of exquisite beauty, brought in more by accident than by necessity. Montague declares of his son smit with a hopeless passion, which he will not reveal—

> "But he, his own affections' counsellor, ...
> But to himself so secret and so close,
> So far from sounding and discovery,
> As is the bud bit with an envious worm,
> Ere he can spread his sweet leaves to the air,
> Or dedicate his beauty to the sun."

This casual description is as full of passionate beauty as when Romeo dwells in frantic fondness on "the white wonder of his Juliet's hand." The reader may, if he pleases, contrast the exquisite pastoral simplicity of the above lines with the gorgeous description of Juliet when Romeo first sees her at her father's house, surrounded by company and artificial splendour.

> "What lady is that which doth enrich the hand
> Of yonder knight? ...
> O! she doth teach the torches to burn bright.
> It seems she hangs upon the cheek of night
> Like a rich jewel in an Ethiop's ear;"

It would be hard to say which of the two garden scenes is the finest, that where he first converses with his love, or takes leave of her the morning after their marriage. Both are like a heaven upon earth; the blissful bowers of Paradise let down upon this lower world. We will give only one passage of these well known scenes to shew the perfect refinement and delicacy of Shakespear's conception of the female character. It is wonderful how Collins, who was a critic and a poet of great sensibility, should have encouraged the common error on this subject by saying—"But stronger Shakespear felt for man alone."

The passage we mean is Juliet's apology for her maiden boldness.

> "Thou know'st the mask of night is on my face.
> Else would a maiden blush bepaint my cheek
> For that which thou hast heard me speak to-night.
> Fain would I dwell on form, fain, fain deny
> What I have spoke: but farewell compliment!

Dost thou love me? I know thou wilt say "Ay";
And I will take thy word; yet, if thou swear'st,
Thou mayst prove false; at lovers' perjuries,
They say, Jove laughs. O gentle Romeo!
If thou dost love, pronounce it faithfully:
Or if thou think'st I am too quickly won,
I'll frown and be perverse and say thee nay,
So thou wilt woo; but else, not for the world.
In truth, fair Montague, I am too fond,
And therefore thou mayst think my haviour light:
But trust me, gentleman, I'll prove more true
Than those that have more cunning to be strange.
I should have been more strange, I must confess,
But that thou over-heard'st, ere I was ware,
My true love's passion: therefore pardon me,
And not impute this yielding to light love,
Which the dark night hath so discovered."

In this and all the rest, her heart, fluttering between pleasure, hope, and fear, seems to have dictated to her tongue, and "calls true love spoken simple modesty." Of the same sort, but bolder in virgin innocence, is her soliloquy after her marriage with Romeo.

"Gallop apace, you fiery-footed steeds,
Towards Phœbus' lodging; such a waggoner
As Phaethon would whip you to the west,
And bring in cloudy night immediately.
Spread thy close curtain, love-performing night!
That runaway's eyes may wink, and Romeo
Leap to these arms, untalk'd of and unseen!
Lovers can see to do their amorous rites
By their own beauties; or, if love be blind,
It best agrees with night. Come, civil night,
Thou sober-suited matron, all in black,
And learn me how to lose a winning match,
Play'd for a pair of stainless maidenhoods:
Hood my unmann'd blood, bating in my cheeks,
With thy black mantle; till strange love, grown bold,
Think true love acted simple modesty.
Come, night! come, Romeo! come, thou day in night!

For thou wilt lie upon the wings of night,
Whiter than new snow on a raven's back.
Come, gentle night; come, loving, black-brow'd night,
Give me my Romeo: and, when he shall die,
Take him and cut him out in little stars,
And he will make the face of heaven so fine
That all the world will be in love with night,
And pay no worship to the garish sun.
O! I have bought the mansion of love,
But not possess'd it, and, though I am sold,
Not yet enjoy'd. So tedious is this day
As is the night before some festival
To an impatient child that hath new robes
And may not wear them."

We rather insert this passage here, inasmuch as we have no doubt it has been expunged from the Family Shakespear. Such critics do not perceive that the feelings of the heart sanctify, without disguising, the impulses of nature. Without refinement themselves, they confound modesty with hypocrisy. Not so the German critic, Schlegel. Speaking of *Romeo and Juliet,* he says, "It was reserved for Shakespear to unite purity of heart and the glow of imagination, sweetness and dignity of manners and passionate violence, in one ideal picture." The character is indeed one of perfect truth and sweetness. It has nothing forward, nothing coy, nothing affected or coquettish about it;—it is a pure effusion of nature. It is as frank as it is modest, for it has no thought that it wishes to conceal. It reposes in conscious innocence on the strength of its affections. Its delicacy does not consist in coldness and reserve, but in combining warmth of imagination and tenderness of heart with the most voluptuous sensibility. Love is a gentle flame that rarifies and expands her whole being. What an idea of trembling haste and airy grace, borne upon the thoughts of love, does the Friar's exclamation give of her, as she approaches his cell to be married—

"Here comes the lady: O!, so light a foot
Will ne'er wear out the everlasting flint:
A lover may bestride the gossamer
That idles in the wanton summer air,
And yet not fall; so light is vanity."

The tragic part of this character is of a piece with the rest. It is the heroic founded on tenderness and delicacy. Of this kind are her resolution to follow the Friar's advice, and the conflict in her bosom between apprehension and love when she comes to take the sleeping poison. Shakespear is blamed for the mixture of low characters. If this is a deformity, it is the source of a thousand beauties. One instance is the contrast between the guileless simplicity of Juliet's attachment to her first love, and the convenient policy of the nurse in advising her to marry Paris, which excites such indignation in her mistress. "Ancient damnation! oh most wicked fiend," etc.

Romeo is Hamlet in love. There is the same rich exuberance of passion and sentiment in the one, that there is of thought and sentiment in the other. Both are absent and self-involved, both live out of themselves in a world of imagination. Hamlet is abstracted from every thing; Romeo is abstracted from every thing but his love, and lost in it. His "frail thoughts dally with faint surmise," and are fashioned out of the suggestions of hope, "the flatteries of sleep." He is himself only in his Juliet; she is his only reality, his heart's true home and idol. The rest of the world is to him a passing dream. How finely is this character portrayed where he recollects himself on seeing Paris slain at the tomb of Juliet!—

> "What said my man when my betossed soul
> Did not attend him as we rode? I think
> He told me Paris should have married Juliet."

And again, just before he hears the sudden tidings of her death—

> "If I may trust the flattering truth of sleep,
> My dreams presage some joyful news at hand:
> My bosom's lord sits lightly on his throne;
> And all this day an unaccustom'd spirit
> Lifts me above the ground with cheerful thoughts.
> I dreamt my lady came and found me dead;—
> Strange dream, that gives a dead man leave to think,—
> And breath'd such life with kisses in my lips,
> That I reviv'd and was an emperor.
> Ah me! how sweet is love itself possess'd,
> When but love's shadows are so rich in joy!"

Romeo's passion for Juliet is not a first love: it succeeds and drives out his passion for another mistress, Rosaline, as the sun hides the stars. This is perhaps an artifice (not absolutely necessary) to give us a higher opinion of the lady, while the first absolute surrender of her heart to him enhances the richness of the prize. The commencement, progress, and ending of his second passion are however complete in themselves, not injured if they are not bettered by the first. The outline of the play is taken from an Italian novel; but the dramatic arrangement of the different scenes between the lovers, the more than dramatic interest in the progress of the story, the development of the characters with time and circumstances, just according to the degree and kind of interest excited, are not inferior to the expression of passion and nature. It has been ingeniously remarked among other proofs of skill in the contrivance of the fable, that the improbability of the main incident in the piece, the administering of the sleeping-potion, is softened and obviated from the beginning by the introduction of the Friar on his first appearance culling simples and descanting on their virtues. Of the passionate scenes in this tragedy, that between the Friar and Romeo when he is told of his sentence of banishment, that between Juliet and the nurse when she hears of it, and of the death of her cousin Tybalt (which bear no proportion in her mind, when passion after the first shock of surprise throws its weight into the scale of her affections) and the last scene at the tomb, are among the most natural and over-powering. In all of these it is not merely the force of any one passion that is given, but the slightest and most unlooked-for transitions from one to another, the mingling currents of every different feeling rising up and prevailing in turn, swayed by the master-mind of the poet, as the waves undulate beneath the gliding storm. Thus when Juliet has by her complaints encouraged the nurse to say, "Shame come to Romeo," she instantly repels the wish, which she had herself occasioned, by answering—

> "Blister'd be thy tongue
> For such a wish! he was not born to shame:
> Upon his brow shame is asham'd to sit;
> For 'tis a throne where honour may be crown'd
> Sole monarch of the universal earth.
> O! what a beast was I to chide at him.
>> *Nurse.* Will you speak well of him that kill'd your cousin?

> *Juliet.* Shall I speak ill of him that is my husband?
> Ah! my poor lord, what tongue shall smooth thy name,
> When I, thy three-hours wife, have mangled it?"

And then follows on the neck of her remorse and returning fondness, that wish treading almost on the brink of impiety, but still held back by the strength of her devotion to her lord, that "father, mother, nay, or both were dead," rather than Romeo banished. If she requires any other excuse, it is in the manner in which Romeo echoes her frantic grief and disappointment in the next scene at being banished from her.—Perhaps one of the finest pieces of acting that ever was witnessed on the stage, is Mr. Kean's manner of doing this scene and his repetition of the word, *Banished*. He treads close indeed upon the genius of his author.

A passage which this celebrated actor and able commentator on Shakespear (actors are the best commentators on the poets) did not give with equal truth or force of feeling was the one which Romeo makes at the tomb of Juliet, before he drinks the poison.

> ———"Let me peruse this face—
> Mercutio's kinsman! noble county Paris!
> What said my man, when my betossed soul
> Did not attend him as we rode? I think,
> He told me Paris should have married Juliet:
> Said he not so? or did I dream it so?
> Or am I mad, hearing him talk of Juliet,
> To think it was so?———O! give me thy hand,
> One writ with me in sour misfortune's book!
> I'll bury thee in a triumphant grave———
> For here lies Juliet.

> ———O, my love! my wife!
> Death that hath suck'd the honey of thy breath,
> Hath had no power yet upon thy beauty:
> Thou art not conquer'd; beauty's ensign yet
> Is crimson in thy lips, and in thy cheeks,
> And Death's pale flag is not advanced there.———
> Tybalt, ly'st thou there in thy bloody sheet?
> O, what more favour can I do to thee,
> Than with that hand that cut thy youth in twain,
> To sunder his that was thine enemy?

Forgive me, cousin! Ah, dear Juliet,
Why art thou yet so fair! Shall I believe
That unsubstantial death is amorous;
And that the lean abhorred monster keeps
Thee here in dark to be his paramour!
For fear of that, I will stay still with thee;
And never from this palace of dim night
Depart again: here, here will I remain
With worms that are thy chamber-maids; O, here
Will I set up my everlasting rest;
And shake the yoke of inauspicious stars
From this world-wearied flesh.—Eyes, look your last!
Arms, take your last embrace! and lips, O you,
The doors of breath, seal with a righteous kiss
A dateless bargain to engrossing death!——
Come, bitter conduct, come unsavoury guide!
Thou desperate pilot, now at once run on
The dashing rocks my sea-sick weary bark!
Here's to my love!—[*Drinks.*] O, true apothecary!
Thy drugs are quick.—Thus with a kiss I die."

    The lines in this speech, describing the loveliness of Juliet, who is sup-
posed to be dead, have been compared to those in which it is said of
Cleopatra after her death, that she looked "as she would take another
Antony in her strong toil of grace"; and a question has been started which
is the finest, that we do not pretend to decide. We can more easily decide between Shakespear and any other author, than between him and
himself.—Shall we quote any more passages to shew his genius or the
beauty of *Romeo and Juliet?* At that rate, we might quote the whole. The
late Mr. Sheridan, on being shewn a volume of the Beauties of Shakespear, very properly asked—"But where are the other eleven?"

Romeo

and

Juliet

CAST OF CHARACTERS

ESCALUS, *Prince of Verona*
PARIS, *a young Nobleman, Kinsman to the Prince*
MONTAGUE } *Heads of two Houses at variance*
CAPULET } *with each other*
Uncle to Capulet
ROMEO, *son to Montague*
MERCUTIO, *Kinsman to the Prince* } *Friends*
BENVOLIO, *Nephew to Montague* } *to Romeo*
TYBALT, *Nephew to Lady Capulet*
FRIAR LAURENCE, *a Franciscan*
FRIAR JOHN, *of the same Order*
BALTHASAR, *Servant to Romeo*
SAMPSON }
GREGORY } *Servants to Capulet*
PETER, *Servant to Juliet's Nurse*
ABRAHAM, *Servant to Montague*
An Apothecary
Three Musicians
Page to Mercutio; Page to Paris; another Page; an Officer
LADY MONTAGUE, *Wife to Montague*
LADY CAPULET, *Wife to Capulet*
JULIET, *Daughter to Capulet*
NURSE to Juliet
CHORUS
Citizens of Verona; male and female Kinsfolk to both Houses; Maskers, Guards, Watchmen, and Attendants

SCENE

Verona; at Mantua.

PROLOGUE

Enter Chorus

CHORUS. Two households, both alike in dignity,
    In fair Verona, where we lay our scene,
From ancient grudge break to new mutiny,
    Where civil blood makes civil hands unclean.
From forth the fatal loins of these two foes
    A pair of star-cross'd lovers take their life;
Whose misadventur'd piteous overthrows
    Do with their death bury their parents' strife.
The fearful passage of their death-mark'd love,
    And the continuance of their parents' rage,
Which, but their children's end, nought could remove,
    Is now the two hours' traffick of our stage;
The which if you with patient ears attend,
What here shall miss, our toil shall strive to mend. *Exit*

ACT ONE

SCENE ONE

Verona. A Public Place.

Enter Sampson and Gregory, armed with swords and bucklers

SAMPSON. Gregory, o' my word, we 'll not carry coals.

GREGORY. No, for then we should be colliers.

SAMPSON. I mean, an we be in choler, we 'll draw.

GREGORY. Ay, while you live, draw your neck out o' the collar.

SAMPSON. I strike quickly, being moved.

GREGORY. But thou art not quickly moved to strike.

SAMPSON. A dog of the house of Montague moves me.

GREGORY. To move is to stir, and to be valiant is to stand; therefore, if thou art moved, thou runnest away.

SAMPSON. A dog of that house shall move me to stand: I will take the wall of any man or maid of Montague's.

GREGORY. That shows thee a weak slave; for the weakest goes to the wall.

SAMPSON. 'Tis true; and therefore women, being the weaker vessels, are ever thrust to the wall: therefore I will push Montague's men from the wall, and thrust his maids to the wall.

GREGORY. The quarrel is between our masters and us their men.

SAMPSON. 'Tis all one, I will show myself a tyrant: when I have fought with the men, I will be cruel with the maids; I will cut off their heads.

GREGORY. The heads of the maids?

SAMPSON. Ay, the heads of the maids, or their maiden-heads; take it in what sense thou wilt.

GREGORY. They must take it in sense that feel it.

SAMPSON. Me they shall feel while I am able to stand; and 'tis known I am a pretty piece of flesh.

GREGORY. 'Tis well thou art not fish; if thou hadst, thou hadst been poor John. Draw thy tool; here comes two of the house of the Montagues.

Enter Abraham and Balthasar

SAMPSON. My naked weapon is out; quarrel, I will back thee.

GREGORY. How! turn thy back and run?

SAMPSON. Fear me not.

GREGORY. No, marry; I fear thee!

SAMPSON. Let us take the law of our sides; let them begin.

GREGORY. I will frown as I pass by, and let them take it as they list.

SAMPSON. Nay, as they dare. I will bite my thumb at them; which is a disgrace to them, if they bear it.

ABRAHAM. Do you bite your thumb at us, sir?

SAMPSON. I do bite my thumb, sir.

ABRAHAM. Do you bite your thumb at us, sir?

SAMPSON. (*Aside to Gregory*) Is the law of our side if I say ay?

GREGORY. (*Aside to Sampson*) No.

SAMPSON. No, sir, I do not bite my thumb at you, sir; but I bite my thumb, sir.

GREGORY. Do you quarrel, sir?

ABRAHAM. Quarrel, sir! no, sir.

SAMPSON. If you do, sir, I am for you: I serve as good a man as you.

ABRAHAM. No better.

SAMPSON. Well, sir.

GREGORY. (*Aside to Sampson*) Say "better"; here comes one of my master's kinsmen.

SAMPSON. Yes, better, sir.

ABRAHAM. You lie.

SAMPSON. Draw, if you be men. Gregory, remember thy swashing blow.

They fight

Enter Benvolio

BENVOLIO. Part, fools!
    Put up your swords; you know not what you do.   *Beats down their swords*

Enter Tybalt

TYBALT. What! art thou drawn among these heartless hinds? Turn thee, Benvolio, look upon thy death.

BENVOLIO. I do but keep the peace: put up thy sword,
    Or manage it to part these men with me.

TYBALT. What! drawn, and talk of peace? I hate the word,

As I hate hell, all Montagues, and thee.
Have at thee, coward!   *They fight*
Enter several persons of both houses, who join the fray;
then enter Citizens, with clubs and partisans
CITIZENS. Clubs, bills, and partisans! strike! beat them down!
Down with the Capulets! down with Montagues!
Enter Capulet in his gown, and Lady Capulet
CAPULET. What noise is this? Give me my long sword, ho!
LADY CAPULET. A crutch, a crutch! Why call you for a sword?
CAPULET. My sword, I say! Old Montague is come,
And flourishes his blade in spite of me.
Enter Montague and Lady Montague
MONTAGUE. Thou villain Capulet! Hold me not; let me go.
LADY MONTAGUE. Thou shalt not stir one foot to seek a foe.
Enter Prince with his Train
PRINCE. Rebellious subjects, enemies to peace,
Profaners of this neighbour-stained steel,—
Will they not hear? What ho! you men, you beasts,
That quench the fire of your pernicious rage
With purple fountains issuing from your veins,
On pain of torture, from those bloody hands
Throw your mis-temper'd weapons to the ground,
And hear the sentence of your moved prince.
Three civil brawls, bred of an airy word,
By thee, old Capulet, and Montague,
Have thrice disturb'd the quiet of our streets,
And made Verona's ancient citizens
Cast by their grave beseeming ornaments,
To wield old partisans, in hands as old,
Canker'd with peace, to part your canker'd hate.
If ever you disturb our streets again
Your lives shall pay the forfeit of the peace.
For this time, all the rest depart away:
You, Capulet, shall go along with me;
And, Montague, come you this afternoon
To know our further pleasure in this case,
To old Free-town, our common judgment-place.
Once more, on pain of death, all men depart.

Exeunt all but Montague, Lady Montague, and Benvolio

MONTAGUE. Who set this ancient quarrel new abroach?
    Speak, nephew, were you by when it began?
BENVOLIO. Here were the servants of your adversary
    And yours close fighting ere I did approach:
    I drew to part them; in the instant came
    The fiery Tybalt, with his sword prepar'd,
    Which, as he breath'd defiance to my ears,
    He swung about his head, and cut the winds,
    Who, nothing hurt withal, hiss'd him in scorn.
    While we were interchanging thrusts and blows,
    Came more and more, and fought on part and part,
    Till the prince came, who parted either part.
LADY MONTAGUE. O! where is Romeo? saw you him to-day?
    Right glad I am he was not at this fray.
BENVOLIO. Madam, an hour before the worshipp'd sun
    Peer'd forth the golden window of the east,
    A troubled mind drave me to walk abroad;
    Where, underneath the grove of sycamore
    That westward rooteth from the city's side,
    So early walking did I see your son:
    Towards him I made; but he was ware of me,
    And stole into the covert of the wood:
    I, measuring his affections by my own,
    That most are busied when they 're most alone,
    Pursu'd my humour not pursuing his,
    And gladly shunn'd who gladly fled from me.
MONTAGUE. Many a morning hath he there been seen,
    With tears augmenting the fresh morning's dew,
    Adding to clouds more clouds with his deep sighs:
    But all so soon as the all-cheering sun
    Should in the furthest east begin to draw
    The shady curtains from Aurora's bed,
    Away from light steals home my heavy son,
    And private in his chamber pens himself,
    Shuts up his windows, locks fair daylight out,
    And makes himself an artificial night.
    Black and portentous must this humour prove
    Unless good counsel may the cause remove.

BENVOLIO. My noble uncle, do you know the cause?
MONTAGUE. I neither know it nor can learn of him.
BENVOLIO. Have you importun'd him by any means?
MONTAGUE. Both by myself and many other friends:
    But he, his own affections' counsellor,
    Is to himself, I will not say how true,
    But to himself so secret and so close,
    So far from sounding and discovery,
    As is the bud bit with an envious worm,
    Ere he can spread his sweet leaves to the air,
    Or dedicate his beauty to the sun.
    Could we but learn from whence his sorrows grow,
    We would as willingly give cure as know.
BENVOLIO. See where he comes: so please you, step aside;
    I'll know his grievance, or be much denied.
MONTAGUE. I would thou wert so happy by thy stay,
    To hear true shrift. Come, madam, let's away.   *Exeunt Montague and Lady*
                                Enter Romeo
BENVOLIO. Good-morrow, cousin.
ROMEO.   Is the day so young?
BENVOLIO. But new struck nine.
ROMEO.   Ay me! sad hours seem long.
    Was that my father that went hence so fast?
BENVOLIO. It was. What sadness lengthens Romeo's hours?
ROMEO. Not having that, which having, makes them short.
BENVOLIO. In love?
ROMEO. Out—
BENVOLIO. Of love?
ROMEO. Out of her favour, where I am in love.
BENVOLIO. Alas! that love, so gentle in his view,
    Should be so tyrannous and rough in proof.
ROMEO. Alas! that love, whose view is muffled still,
    Should, without eyes, see pathways to his will.
    Where shall we dine? O me! What fray was here?
    Yet tell me not, for I have heard it all.
    Here's much to do with hate, but more with love.
    Why then, O brawling love! O loving hate!
    O any thing! of nothing first create.
    O heavy lightness! serious vanity!

Mis-shapen chaos of well-seeming forms!
Feather of lead, bright smoke, cold fire, sick health!
Still-waking sleep, that is not what it is!
This love feel I, that feel no love in this.
Dost thou not laugh?

BENVOLIO.   No, coz, I rather weep.

ROMEO. Good heart, at what?

BENVOLIO. At thy good heart's oppression.

ROMEO. Why, such is love's transgression.
Griefs of mine own lie heavy in my breast,
Which thou wilt propagate to have it press'd
With more of thine: this love that thou hast shown
Doth add more grief to too much of mine own.
Love is a smoke rais'd with the fume of sighs;
Being purg'd, a fire sparkling in lovers' eyes;
Being vex'd, a sea nourish'd with lovers' tears:
What is it else? a madness most discreet,
A choking gall, and a preserving sweet.
Farewell, my coz.   *Going*

BENVOLIO.   Soft, I will go along;
An if you leave me so, you do me wrong.

ROMEO. Tut! I have lost myself; I am not here;
This is not Romeo, he's some other where.

BENVOLIO. Tell me in sadness, who is that you love.

ROMEO. What! shall I groan and tell thee?

BENVOLIO.   Groan! why, no;
But sadly tell me who.

ROMEO. Bid a sick man in sadness make his will;
Ah! word ill urg'd to one that is so ill.
In sadness, cousin, I do love a woman.

BENVOLIO. I aim'd so near when I suppos'd you lov'd.

ROMEO. A right good mark-man! And she's fair I love.

BENVOLIO. A right fair mark, fair coz, is soonest hit.

ROMEO. Well, in that hit you miss: she'll not be hit
With Cupid's arrow; she hath Dian's wit;
And, in strong proof of chastity well arm'd,
From love's weak childish bow she lives unharm'd.
She will not stay the siege of loving terms,
Nor bide the encounter of assailing eyes,

Nor ope her lap to saint-seducing gold:
O! she is rich in beauty; only poor
That, when she dies, with beauty dies her store.
BENVOLIO. Then she hath sworn that she will still live chaste?
ROMEO. She hath, and in that sparing makes huge waste;
For beauty, starv'd with her severity,
Cuts beauty off from all posterity.
She is too fair, too wise, wisely too fair,
To merit bliss by making me despair:
She hath forsworn to love, and in that vow
Do I live dead that live to tell it now.
BENVOLIO. Be rul'd by me; forget to think of her.
ROMEO. O! teach me how I should forget to think.
BENVOLIO. By giving liberty unto thine eyes:
Examine other beauties.
ROMEO.   'Tis the way
To call hers exquisite, in question more.
These happy masks that kiss fair ladies' brows
Being black put us in mind they hide the fair:
He, that is strucken blind cannot forget
The precious treasure of his eyesight lost:
Show me a mistress that is passing fair,
What doth her beauty serve but as a note
Where I may read who pass'd that passing fair?
Farewell: thou canst not teach me to forget.
BENVOLIO. I'll pay that doctrine, or else die in debt.   *Exeunt*

SCENE TWO

A Street.
Enter Capulet, Paris, and Servant
CAPULET. But Montague is bound as well as I,
In penalty alike; and 'tis not hard, I think,
For men so old as we to keep the peace.
PARIS. Of honourable reckoning are you both;
And pity 'tis you liv'd at odds so long.
But now, my lord, what say you to my suit?
CAPULET. But saying o'er what I have said before:
My child is yet a stranger in the world,

She hath not seen the change of fourteen years;
Let two more summers wither in their pride
Ere we may think her ripe to be a bride.
PARIS. Younger than she are happy mothers made.
CAPULET. And too soon marr'd are those so early made.
Earth hath swallow'd all my hopes but she,
She is the hopeful lady of my earth:
But woo her, gentle Paris, get her heart,
My will to her consent is but a part;
An she agree, within her scope of choice
Lies my consent and fair according voice.
This night I hold an old accustom'd feast,
Whereto I have invited many a guest
Such as I love; and you, among the store,
Once more, most welcome, makes my number more.
At my poor house look to behold this night
Earth-treading stars that make dark heaven light:
Such comfort as do lusty young men feel
When well-apparell'd April on the heel
Of limping winter treads, even such delight
Among fresh female buds shall you this night
Inherit at my house; hear all, all see,
And like her most whose merit most shall be:
Which on more view, of many mine being one
May stand in number, though in reckoning none.
Come, go with me. (*To Servant, giving him a paper*) Go,
sirrah, trudge about
Through fair Verona; find those persons out
Whose names are written there, and to them say,
My house and welcome on their pleasure stay.   *Exeunt Capulet and Paris*
SERVANT. Find them out whose names are written here! It is written that
the shoemaker should meddle with his yard, and the tailor with his
last, the fisher with his pencil, and the painter with his nets; but I am
sent to find those persons, whose names are here writ, and can never
find what names the writing person hath here writ. I must to the
learned. In good time.

Enter Benvolio and Romeo

BENVOLIO. Tut! man, one fire burns out another's burning.
One pain is lessen'd by another's anguish;

Turn giddy, and be holp by backward turning;
   One desperate grief cures with another's languish:
Take thou some new infection to thy eye,
And the rank poison of the old will die.

ROMEO. Your plantain leaf is excellent for that.

BENVOLIO. For what, I pray thee?

ROMEO.   For your broken shin.

BENVOLIO. Why, Romeo, art thou mad?

ROMEO. Not mad, but bound more than a madman is;
   Shut up in prison, kept without my food,
   Whipp'd and tormented, and—Good den, good fellow.

SERVANT. God gi' good den. I pray, sir, can you read?

ROMEO. Ay, mine own fortune in my misery.

SERVANT. Perhaps you have learn'd it without book: but, I pray, can you
   read any thing you see?

ROMEO. Ay, if I know the letters and the language.

SERVANT. Ye say honestly; rest you merry! *Offering to go*

ROMEO. Stay, fellow; I can read. (*He reads*) "Signior Martino and his wife
   and daughters; County Anselme and his beauteous sisters; the lady
   widow of Vitruvio; Signior Placentio, and his lovely nieces; Mercutio
   and his brother Valentine; mine uncle Capulet, his wife and daughters;
   my fair niece Rosaline; Livia; Signior Valentio and his cousin Tybalt;
   Lucio and the lively Helena."
A fair assembly: whither should they come?

SERVANT. Up.

ROMEO. Whither?

SERVANT. To supper; to our house.

ROMEO. Whose house?

SERVANT. My master's.

ROMEO. Indeed, I should have asked you that before.

SERVANT. Now I'll tell you without asking. My master is the great rich
   Capulet; and if you be not of the house of Montagues, I pray, come
   and crush a cup of wine. Rest you merry!   *Exit*

BENVOLIO. At this same ancient feast of Capulet's,
   Sups the fair Rosaline, whom thou so lov'st,
   With all the admired beauties of Verona:
   Go thither; and, with unattainted eye,
   Compare her face with some that I shall show,
   And I will make thee think thy swan a crow.

ROMEO. When the devout religion of mine eye
    Maintains such falsehood, then turn tears to fires!
And these, who often drown'd could never die,
    Transparent heretics, be burnt for liars!
One fairer than my love! the all-seeing sun
Ne'er saw her match since first the world begun.

BENVOLIO. Tut! you saw her fair, none else being by,
    Herself pois'd with herself in either eye;
But in that crystal scales let there be weigh'd
Your lady's love against some other maid
That I will show you shining at this feast,
And she shall scant show well that now shows best.

ROMEO. I'll go along, no such sight to be shown,
    But to rejoice in splendour of mine own.
                              Exeunt

SCENE THREE

A Room in Capulet's House.

Enter Lady Capulet and Nurse

LADY CAPULET. Nurse, where's my daughter? Call her forth to me.

NURSE. Now, by my maidenhead, at twelve year old,
    I bade her come. What, lamb! what, lady-bird!
God forbid! where's this girl? what, Juliet!

Enter Juliet

JULIET. How now! who calls?

NURSE.   Your mother.

JULIET.   Madam, I am here.
    What is your will?

LADY CAPULET. This is the matter. Nurse, give leave awhile.
    We must talk in secret: nurse, come back again;
I have remember'd me, thou's hear our counsel.
Thou know'st my daughter's of a pretty age.

NURSE. Faith, I can tell her age unto an hour.

LADY CAPULET. She's not fourteen.

NURSE.   I'll lay fourteen of my teeth—
    And yet to my teen be it spoken I have but four—
She is not fourteen. How long is it now
To Lammas-tide?

LADY CAPULET. A fortnight and odd days.

NURSE. Even or odd, of all days in the year,
  Come Lammas-eve at night shall she be fourteen.
  Susan and she—God rest all Christian souls!—
  Were of an age. Well, Susan is with God;
  She was too good for me. But, as I said,
  On Lammas-eve at night shall she be fourteen;
  That shall she, marry; I remember it well.
  'Tis since the earthquake now eleven years;
  And she was wean'd, I never shall forget it,
  Of all the days of the year, upon that day;
  For I had then laid wormwood to my dug,
  Sitting in the sun under the dove-house wall;
  My lord and you were then at Mantua.
  Nay, I do bear a brain:—but, as I said,
  When it did taste the wormwood on the nipple
  Of my dug and felt it bitter, pretty fool!
  To see it tetchy and fall out with the dug.
  "Shake," quoth the dove-house: 'twas no need, I trow,
  To bid me trudge:
  And since that time it is eleven years;
  For then she could stand high lone; nay, by the rood,
  She could have run and waddled all about;
  For even the day before she broke her brow:
  And then my husband—God be with his soul!
  A' was a merry man—took up the child:
  "Yea," quoth he, "dost thou fall upon thy face?
  Thou wilt fall backward when thou hast more wit;
  Wilt thou not, Jule?" and, by my halidom,
  The pretty wretch left crying, and said "Ay."
  To see now how a jest shall come about!
  I warrant, an I should live a thousand years,
  I never should forget it: "Wilt thou not, Jule?" quoth he;
  And, pretty fool, it stinted and said "Ay."
LADY CAPULET. Enough of this; I pray thee, hold thy peace.
NURSE. Yes, madam. Yet I cannot choose but laugh,
  To think it should leave crying, and say "Ay."
  And yet, I warrant, it had upon its brow
  A bump as big as a young cockerel's stone;
  A parlous knock; and it cried bitterly:

"Yea," quoth my husband, "fall'st upon thy face?
Thou wilt fall backward when thou com'st to age;
Wilt thou not, Jule?" it stinted and said "Ay."
JULIET. And stint thou too, I pray thee, nurse, say I.
NURSE. Peace, I have done. God mark thee to his grace!
Thou wast the prettiest babe that e'er I nursed:
An I might live to see thee married once,
I have my wish.
LADY CAPULET. Marry, that "marry" is the very theme
I came to talk of. Tell me, daughter Juliet,
How stands your disposition to be married?
JULIET. It is an honour that I dream not of.
NURSE. An honour! were not I thine only nurse,
I would say thou hadst suck'd wisdom from thy teat.
LADY CAPULET. Well, think of marriage now; younger than you,
Here in Verona, ladies of esteem,
Are made already mothers: by my count,
I was your mother much upon these years
That you are now a maid. Thus then in brief,
The valiant Paris seeks you for his love.
NURSE. A man, young lady! lady, such a man
As all the world—why, he's a man of wax.
LADY CAPULET. Verona's summer hath not such a flower.
NURSE. Nay, he's a flower; in faith, a very flower.
LADY CAPULET. What say you? can you love the gentleman?
This night you shall behold him at our feast;
Read o'er the volume of young Paris' face
And find delight writ there with beauty's pen;
Examine every married lineament,
And see how one another lends content;
And what obscur'd in this fair volume lies
Find written in the margent of his eyes.
This precious book of love, this unbound lover,
To beautify him, only lacks a cover:
The fish lives in the sea, and 'tis much pride
For fair without the fair within to hide:
That book in many eyes doth share the glory,
That in gold clasps locks in the golden story:

So shall you share all that he doth possess,
By having him making yourself no less.
NURSE. No less! nay, bigger; women grow by men.
LADY CAPULET. Speak briefly, can you like of Paris' love?
JULIET. I 'll look to like, if looking liking move;
But no more deep will I endart mine eye
Than your consent gives strength to make it fly.

Enter a Servant

SERVANT. Madam, the guests are come, supper served up, you called, my
young lady asked for, the nurse cursed in the pantry, and everything in
extremity. I must hence to wait; I beseech you, follow straight.
LADY CAPULET. We follow thee. Juliet, the county stays.
NURSE. Go, girl, seek happy nights to happy days.   *Exeunt*

SCENE FOUR

A Street.

*Enter Romeo, Mercutio, Benvolio, with five or six
Maskers, Torchbearers, and Others*

ROMEO. What! shall this speech be spoke for our excuse,
Or shall we on without apology?
BENVOLIO. The date is out of such prolixity:
We'll have no Cupid hood-wink'd with a scarf,
Bearing a Tartar's painted bow of lath,
Scaring the ladies like a crow-keeper;
Nor no without-book prologue, faintly spoke
After the prompter, for our entrance:
But, let them measure us by what they will,
We'll measure them a measure, and be gone.
ROMEO. Give me a torch: I am not for this ambling;
Being but heavy, I will bear the light.
MERCUTIO. Nay, gentle Romeo, we must have you dance.
ROMEO. Not I, believe me; you have dancing shoes
With nimble soles; I have a soul of lead
So stakes me to the ground I cannot move.
MERCUTIO. You are a lover; borrow Cupid's wings,
And soar with them above a common bound.
ROMEO. I am too sore enpierced with his shaft

To soar with his light feathers; and so bound
I cannot bound a pitch above dull woe:
Under love's heavy burden do I sink.

MERCUTIO. And, to sink in it, should you burden love;
Too great oppression for a tender thing.

ROMEO. Is love a tender thing? it is too rough,
Too rude, too boisterous; and it pricks like thorn.

MERCUTIO. If love be rough with you, be rough with love;
Prick love for pricking, and you beat love down.
Give me a case to put my visage in: *Putting on a mask*
A visor for a visor! what care I,
What curious eye doth quote deformities?
Here are the beetle brows shall blush for me.

BENVOLIO. Come, knock and enter; and no sooner in,
But every man betake him to his legs.

ROMEO. A torch for me; let wantons, light of heart,
Tickle the senseless rushes with their heels,
For I am proverb'd with a grandsire phrase;
I'll be a candle-holder, and look on.
The game was ne'er so fair, and I am done.

MERCUTIO. Tut! dun's the mouse, the constable's own word:
If thou art Dun, we 'll draw thee from the mire,
Of—save your reverence—love, wherein thou stick'st
Up to the ears. Come, we burn daylight, ho!

ROMEO. Nay, that's not so.

MERCUTIO.   I mean, sir, in delay
We waste our lights in vain, like lamps by day.
Take our good meaning, for our judgment sits
Five times in that ere once in our five wits.

ROMEO. And we mean well in going to this mask;
But 'tis no wit to go.

MERCUTIO.   Why, may one ask?

ROMEO. I dream'd a dream to-night.

MERCUTIO.   And so did I.

ROMEO. Well, what was yours?

MERCUTIO.   That dreamers often lie.

ROMEO. In bed asleep, while they do dream things true.

MERCUTIO. O! then, I see, Queen Mab hath been with you.

BENVOLIO. Queen Mab! What's she?

MERCUTIO. She is the fairies' midwife, and she comes
   In shape no bigger than an agate-stone
   On the fore-finger of an alderman,
   Drawn with a team of little atomies
   Athwart men's noses as they lie asleep:
   Her waggon-spokes made of long spinners' legs;
   The cover, of the wings of grasshoppers;
   The traces, of the smallest spider's web;
   The collars, of the moonshine's watery beams;
   Her whip, of cricket's bone; the lash, of film;
   Her waggoner, a small grey-coated gnat,
   Not half so big as a round little worm
   Prick'd from the lazy finger of a maid;
   Her chariot is an empty hazel-nut,
   Made by the joiner squirrel or old grub,
   Time out o' mind the fairies' coach-makers.
   And in this state she gallops night by night
   Through lovers' brains, and then they dream of love;
   O'er courtiers' knees, that dream on curtsies straight;
   O'er lawyers' fingers, who straight dream on fees;
   O'er ladies' lips, who straight on kisses dream;
   Which oft the angry Mab with blisters plagues,
   Because their breaths with sweetmeats tainted are.
   Sometimes she gallops o'er a courtier's nose,
   And then dreams he of smelling out a suit;
   And sometimes comes she with a tithe-pig's tail,
   Tickling a parson's nose as a' lies asleep,
   Then dreams he of another benefice;
   Sometimes she driveth o'er a soldier's neck,
   And then dreams he of cutting foreign throats,
   Of breaches, ambuscadoes, Spanish blades,
   Of healths five fathom deep; and then anon
   Drums in his ear, at which he starts and wakes;
   And, being thus frighted, swears a prayer or two,
   And sleeps again. This is that very Mab
   That plats the manes of horses in the night;
   And bakes the elf-locks in foul sluttish hairs,
   Which once untangled much misfortune bodes;
   This is the hag, when maids lie on their backs,

That presses them and learns them first to bear,
Making them women of good carriage:
This is she—
ROMEO.   Peace, peace! Mercutio, peace!
Thou talk'st of nothing.
MERCUTIO.   True, I talk of dreams,
Which are the children of an idle brain,
Begot of nothing but vain fantasy;
Which is as thin of substance as the air,
And more inconstant than the wind, who woos
Even now the frozen bosom of the north,
And, being anger'd, puffs away from thence,
Turning his face to the dew-dropping south.
BENVOLIO. This wind you talk of blows us from ourselves;
Supper is done, and we shall come too late.
ROMEO. I fear too early; for my mind misgives
Some consequence yet hanging in the stars
Shall bitterly begin his fearful date
With this night's revels, and expire the term
Of a despised life clos'd in my breast
By some vile forfeit of untimely death.
But he, that hath the steerage of my course,
Direct my sail! On, lusty gentlemen.
BENVOLIO. Strike, drum.   *Exeunt*

SCENE FIVE

A Hall in Capulet's House.
Musicians waiting. Enter Servingmen

FIRST SERVINGMAN. Where's Potpan, that he helps not to take away? he
shift a trencher! he scrape a trencher!
SECOND SERVINGMAN. When good manners shall lie all in one or two
men's hands, and they unwashed too, 'tis a foul thing.
FIRST SERVINGMAN. Away with the joint-stools, remove the court-
cupboard, look to the plate. Good thou, save me a piece of marchpane;
and, as thou lovest me, let the porter let in Susan Grindstone and Nell.
Antony! and Potpan!
SECOND SERVINGMAN. Ay, boy; ready.

FIRST SERVINGMAN. You are looked for and called for, asked for and
  sought for in the great chamber.
THIRD SERVINGMAN. We cannot be here and there too.
SECOND SERVINGMAN. Cheerly, boys; be brisk awhile, and the longer
  liver take all.   *They retire behind*

  Enter Capulet and Juliet and Others of his house,
  meeting the Guests and Maskers

CAPULET. Welcome, gentlemen! ladies that have their toes
  Unplagu'd with corns will walk a bout with you.
  Ah ha! my mistresses, which of you all
  Will now deny to dance? she that makes dainty, she,
  I'll swear, hath corns; am I come near ye now?
  Welcome, gentlemen! I have seen the day
  That I have worn a visor, and could tell
  A whispering tale in a fair lady's ear
  Such as would please; 'tis gone, 'tis gone, 'tis gone.
  You are welcome, gentlemen! Come, musicians, play.
  A hall! a hall! give room, and foot it, girls.   *Music plays, and they dance*
  More light, ye knaves! and turn the tables up,
  And quench the fire, the room has grown too hot.
  Ah! sirrah, this unlook'd-for sport comes well.
  Nay, sit, nay, sit, good cousin Capulet,
  For you and I are past our dancing days;
  How long is 't now since last yourself and I
  Were in a mask?
SECOND CAPULET. By 'r Lady, thirty years.
CAPULET. What, man! 'tis not so much, 'tis not so much:
  'Tis since the nuptial of Lucentio,
  Come Pentecost as quickly as it will,
  Some five and twenty years; and then we mask'd.
SECOND CAPULET. 'Tis more, 'tis more; his son is elder, sir.
  His son is thirty.
CAPULET. Will you tell me that?
  His son was but a ward two years ago.
ROMEO. What lady is that which doth enrich the hand
  Of yonder knight?
SERVINGMAN. I know not, sir.
ROMEO. O! she doth teach the torches to burn bright.

It seems she hangs upon the cheek of night
Like a rich jewel in an Ethiop's ear;
Beauty too rich for use, for earth too dear!
So shows a snowy dove trooping with crows,
As yonder lady o'er her fellows shows.
The measure done, I'll watch her place of stand,
And, touching hers, make blessed my rude hand.
Did my heart love till now? forswear it, sight!
For I ne'er saw true beauty till this night.

TYBALT. This, by his voice, should be a Montague.
Fetch me my rapier, boy. What! dares the slave
Come hither, cover'd with an antick face,
To fleer and scorn at our solemnity?
Now, by the stock and honour of my kin,
To strike him dead I hold it not a sin.

CAPULET. Why, how now, kinsman! wherefore storm you so?

TYBALT. Uncle, this is a Montague, our foe;
A villain that is hither come in spite,
To scorn at our solemnity this night.

CAPULET. Young Romeo, is it?

TYBALT.   'Tis he, that villain Romeo.

CAPULET. Content thee, gentle coz, let him alone:
He bears him like a portly gentleman;
And, to say truth, Verona brags of him
To be a virtuous and well-govern'd youth.
I would not for the wealth of all this town
Here in my house do him disparagement;
Therefore be patient, take no note of him:
It is my will; the which if thou respect,
Show a fair presence and put off these frowns,
An ill-beseeming semblance for a feast.

TYBALT. It fits, when such a villain is a guest:
I'll not endure him.

CAPULET.   He shall be endur'd:
What! goodman boy; I say, he shall, go to;
Am I the master here, or you? go to.
You'll not endure him! God shall mend my soul!
You'll make a mutiny among my guests!
You will set cock-a-hoop! you'll be the man!

TYBALT. Why, uncle, 'tis a shame.
CAPULET.   Go to, go to;
  You are a saucy boy—is 't so indeed?—
  This trick may chance to scathe you.—I know what:
  You must contrary me! marry, 'tis time.
  Well said, my hearts! You are a princox; go:
  Be quiet, or—More light, more light!—For shame!
  I'll make you quiet. What! cheerly, my hearts!
TYBALT. Patience perforce with wilful choler meeting
  Makes my flesh tremble in their different greeting.
  I will withdraw; but this intrusion shall
  Now seeming sweet convert to bitter gall.   *Exit*
ROMEO. (*To Juliet*) If I profane with my unworthiest hand
  This holy shrine, the gentle sin is this;
  My lips, two blushing pilgrims, ready stand
  To smooth that rough touch with a tender kiss.
JULIET. Good pilgrim, you do wrong your hand too much,
  Which mannerly devotion shows in this;
  For saints have hands that pilgrims' hands do touch,
      And palm to palm is holy palmer's kiss.
ROMEO. Have not saints lips, and holy palmers too?
JULIET. Ay, pilgrim, lips that they must use in prayer.
ROMEO. O! then, dear saint, let lips do what hands do;
  They pray, grant thou, lest faith turn to despair.
JULIET. Saints do not move, though grant for prayer's sake.
ROMEO. Then move not, while my prayers' effect I take.
  Thus from my lips, by thine, my sin is purg'd.   *Kissing her*
JULIET. Then have my lips the sin that they have took.
ROMEO. Sin from my lips? O trespass sweetly urg'd!
  Give me my sin again.
JULIET.   You kiss by the book.
NURSE. Madam, your mother craves a word with you.
ROMEO. What is her mother?
NURSE.   Marry, bachelor,
  Her mother is the lady of the house,
  And a good lady, and a wise, and virtuous:
  I nurs'd her daughter, that you talk'd withal;
  I tell you he that can lay hold of her
  Shall have the chinks.

ROMEO. Is she a Capulet?
O dear account! my life is my foe's debt.

BENVOLIO. Away, be gone; the sport is at the best.

ROMEO. Ay, so I fear; the more is my unrest.

CAPULET. Nay, gentlemen, prepare not to be gone;
We have a trifling foolish banquet towards.
Is it e'en so? Why then, I thank you all;
I thank you, honest gentlemen; good-night.
More torches here! Come on then, let's to bed.
Ah! sirrah, by my fay, it waxes late;
I'll to my rest. *Exeunt all except Juliet and Nurse*

JULIET. Come hither, nurse. What is yond gentleman?

NURSE. The son and heir of old Tiberio.

JULIET. What's he that now is going out of door?

NURSE. Marry, that, I think, be young Petruchio.

JULIET. What's he, that follows there that would not dance?

NURSE. I know not.

JULIET. Go, ask his name.—If he be married,
My grave is like to be my wedding-bed.

NURSE. His name is Romeo, and a Montague;
The only son of your great enemy.

JULIET. My only love sprung from my only hate!
Too early seen unknown, and known too late!
Prodigious birth of love it is to me,
That I must love a loathed enemy.

NURSE. What's this, What's this?

JULIET. A rime I learn'd even now
Of one I danc'd withal. *One calls within, "Juliet!"*

NURSE. Anon, anon!—
Come, let's away; the strangers are all gone. *Exeunt*

ACT TWO

PROLOGUE

Enter Chorus

CHORUS. Now old desire doth in his death-bed lie,
  And young affection gapes to be his heir;
That fair for which love groan'd for and would die,
  With tender Juliet match'd, is now not fair.
Now Romeo is belov'd and loves again,
  Alike bewitched by the charm of looks,
But to his foe suppos'd he must complain,
  And she steal love's sweet bait from fearful hooks:
Being held a foe, he may not have access
  To breathe such vows as lovers us'd to swear;
And she as much in love, her means much less
  To meet her new-beloved any where:
But passion lends them power, time means, to meet,
Tempering extremity with extreme sweet.   *Exit*

SCENE ONE

Verona. A Lane by the Wall of Capulet's Orchard.

Enter Romeo

ROMEO. Can I go forward when my heart is here?
  Turn back, dull earth, and find thy centre out.

He climbs the wall, and leaps down within it
Enter Benvolio and Mercutio

BENVOLIO. Romeo! my cousin Romeo!

MERCUTIO.   He is wise;
   And, on my life, hath stol'n him home to bed.
BENVOLIO. He ran this way, and leap'd this orchard wall:
   Call, good Mercutio.
MERCUTIO.   Nay, I'll conjure too.
   Romeo! humours! madman! passion! lover!
   Appear thou in the likeness of a sigh:
   Speak but one rime and I am satisfied;
   Cry but "Ay me!" couple but "love" and "dove";
   Speak to my gossip Venus one fair word,
   One nickname for her purblind son and heir,
   Young Adam Cupid, he that shot so trim
   When King Cophetua lov'd the beggar-maid.
   He heareth not, he stirreth not, he moveth not;
   The ape is dead, and I must conjure him.
   I conjure thee by Rosaline's bright eyes,
   By her high forehead, and her scarlet lip,
   By her fine foot, straight leg, and quivering thigh,
   And the demesnes that there adjacent lie,
   That in thy likeness thou appear to us.
BENVOLIO. An if he hear thee, thou wilt anger him.
MERCUTIO. This cannot anger him: 'twould anger him
   To raise a spirit in his mistress' circle
   Of some strange nature, letting it there stand
   Till she had laid it, and conjur'd it down;
   That were some spite: my invocation
   Is fair and honest, and in his mistress' name
   I conjure only but to raise up him.
BENVOLIO. Come, he hath hid himself among these trees,
   To be consorted with the humorous night:
   Blind is his love and best befits the dark.
MERCUTIO. If love be blind, love cannot hit the mark.
   Now will he sit under a medlar tree,
   And wish his mistress were that kind of fruit
   As maids call medlars, when they laugh alone.
   O Romeo! that she were, O! that she were
   An open "et cætera," thou a poperin pear.
   Romeo, good-night: I'll to my truckle-bed;

This field-bed is too cold for me to sleep:
Come, shall we go?

BENVOLIO.   Go, then; for 'tis in vain
To seek him here that means not to be found.   *Exeunt*

SCENE TWO

Capulet's Orchard.

Enter Romeo

ROMEO. He jests at scars, that never felt a wound.

Juliet appears above at a window

But, soft! what light through yonder window breaks?
It is the east, and Juliet is the sun!
Arise, fair sun, and kill the envious moon,
Who is already sick and pale with grief,
That thou her maid art far more fair than she:
Be not her maid, since she is envious;
Her vestal livery is but sick and green,
And none but fools do wear it; cast it off.
It is my lady; O! it is my love:
O! that she knew she were.
She speaks, yet she says nothing: what of that?
Her eye discourses; I will answer it.
I am too bold, 'tis not to me she speaks:
Two of the fairest stars in all the heaven,
Having some business, do entreat her eyes
To twinkle in their spheres till they return.
What if her eyes were there, they in her head?
The brightness of her cheek would shame those stars
As daylight doth a lamp; her eyes in heaven
Would through the airy region stream so bright
That birds would sing and think it were not night.
See! how she leans her cheek upon her hand:
O! that I were a glove upon that hand,
That I might touch that cheek.

JULIET.   Ay me!

ROMEO.   She speaks:
O! speak again, bright angel; for thou art

As glorious to this night, being o'er my head,
As is a winged messenger of heaven
Unto the white-upturned wondering eyes
Of mortals, that fall back to gaze on him
When he bestrides the lazy-pacing clouds,
And sails upon the bosom of the air.

JULIET. O Romeo, Romeo! wherefore art thou Romeo?
    Deny thy father, and refuse thy name;
    Or, if thou wilt not, be but sworn my love,
    And I'll no longer be a Capulet.

ROMEO. (*Aside*) Shall I hear more, or shall I speak at this?

JULIET. 'Tis but thy name that is my enemy;
    Thou art thyself though, not a Montague.
    What's Montague? it is nor hand, nor foot,
    Nor arm, nor face, nor any other part
    Belonging to a man. O! be some other name:
    What's in a name? That which we call a rose
    By any other name would smell as sweet;
    So Romeo would, were he not Romeo call'd,
    Retain that dear perfection which he owes
    Without that title. Romeo, doff thy name;
    And for that name, which is no part of thee,
    Take all myself.

ROMEO.   I take thee at thy word.
    Call me but love, and I'll be new baptiz'd;
    Henceforth I never will be Romeo.

JULIET. What man art thou, that, thus bescreen'd in night,
    So stumblest on my counsel?

ROMEO.   By a name
    I know not how to tell thee who I am:
    My name, dear saint, is hateful to myself,
    Because it is an enemy to thee:
    Had I it written, I would tear the word.

JULIET. My ears have not yet drunk a hundred words
    Of that tongue's uttering, yet I know the sound:
    Art thou not Romeo, and a Montague?

ROMEO. Neither, fair maid, if either thee dislike.

JULIET. How cam'st thou hither, tell me, and wherefore?
    The orchard walls are high and hard to climb,

And the place death, considering who thou art,
If any of my kinsmen find thee here.
ROMEO. With love's light wings did I o'erperch these walls;
    For stony limits cannot hold love out,
    And what love can do that dares love attempt;
    Therefore thy kinsmen are no stop to me.
JULIET. If they do see thee they will murder thee.
ROMEO. Alack! there lies more peril in thine eye
    Than twenty of their swords: look thou but sweet,
    And I am proof against their enmity.
JULIET. I would not for the world they saw thee here.
ROMEO. I have night's cloak to hide me from their eyes;
    And but thou love me, let them find me here;
    My life were better ended by their hate,
    Than death prorogued, wanting of thy love.
JULIET. By whose direction found'st thou out this place?
ROMEO. By Love, that first did prompt me to inquire;
    He lent me counsel, and I lent him eyes.
    I am no pilot; yet wert thou as far
    As that vast shore wash'd with the furthest sea,
    I would adventure for such merchandise.
JULIET. Thou know'st the mask of night is on my face.
    Else would a maiden blush bepaint my cheek
    For that which thou hast heard me speak to-night.
    Fain would I dwell on form, fain, fain deny
    What I have spoke: but farewell compliment!
    Dost thou love me? I know thou wilt say "Ay";
    And I will take thy word; yet, if thou swear'st,
    Thou mayst prove false; at lovers' perjuries,
    They say, Jove laughs. O gentle Romeo!
    If thou dost love, pronounce it faithfully:
    Or if thou think'st I am too quickly won,
    I'll frown and be perverse and say thee nay,
    So thou wilt woo; but else, not for the world.
    In truth, fair Montague, I am too fond,
    And therefore thou mayst think my haviour light:
    But trust me, gentleman, I'll prove more true
    Than those that have more cunning to be strange.
    I should have been more strange, I must confess,

But that thou over-heard'st, ere I was ware,
My true love's passion: therefore pardon me,
And not impute this yielding to light love,
Which the dark night hath so discovered.

ROMEO. Lady, by yonder blessed moon I swear
That tips with silver all these fruit-tree tops,—

JULIET. O! swear not by the moon, the inconstant moon.
That monthly changes in her circled orb,
Lest that thy love prove likewise variable.

ROMEO. What shall I swear by?

JULIET.   Do not swear at all;
Or, if thou wilt, swear by thy gracious self,
Which is the god of my idolatry,
And I'll believe thee.

ROMEO.   If my heart's dear love—

JULIET. Well, do not swear. Although I joy in thee,
I have no joy of this contract to-night:
It is too rash, too unadvis'd, too sudden;
Too like the lightning, which doth cease to be
Ere one can say it lightens. Sweet, good-night!
This but of love, by summer's ripening breath,
May prove a beauteous flower when next we meet.
Good-night, good-night! as sweet repose and rest
Come to thy heart as that within my breast!

ROMEO. O! wilt thou leave me so unsatisfied?

JULIET. What satisfaction canst thou have to-night?

ROMEO. The exchange of thy love's faithful vow for mine.

JULIET. I gave thee mine before thou didst request it;
And yet I would it were to give again.

ROMEO. Wouldst thou withdraw it? for what purpose, love?

JULIET. But to be frank, and give it thee again.
And yet I wish but for the thing I have:
My bounty is as boundless as the sea,
My love as deep; the more I give to thee,
The more I have, for both are infinite.   *Nurse calls within*
I hear some noise within; dear love, adieu!
Anon, good nurse! Sweet Montague, be true.
Stay but a little, I will come again.   *Exit above*

ROMEO. O blessed, blessed night! I am afeard,

Being in night, all this is but a dream,
Too flattering-sweet to be substantial.

Re-enter Juliet, above

JULIET. Three words, dear Romeo, and good-night indeed.
If that thy bent of love be honourable,
Thy purpose marriage, send me word to-morrow,
By one that I'll procure to come to thee,
Where, and what time, thou wilt perform the rite;
And all my fortunes at thy foot I'll lay,
And follow thee my lord throughout the world.

NURSE. (*Within*) Madam!

JULIET. I come, anon.—But if thou mean'st not well, I do beseech thee,—

NURSE. (*Within*) Madam!

JULIET.   By and by; I come;—
To cease thy suit, and leave me to my grief:
To-morrow will I send.

ROMEO.   So thrive my soul,—

JULIET. A thousand times good-night!   *Exit above*

ROMEO. A thousand times the worse, to want thy light.
Love goes toward love, as schoolboys from their books;
But love from love, toward school with heavy looks.   *Retiring*

Re-enter Juliet, above

JULIET. Hist! Romeo, hist! O! for a falconer's voice,
To lure this tassel-gentle back again.
Bondage is hoarse, and may not speak aloud,
Else would I tear the cave where Echo lies,
And make her airy tongue more hoarse than mine,
With repetition of my Romeo's name.

ROMEO. It is my soul that calls upon my name:
How silver-sweet sound lovers' tongues by night,
Like softest music to attending ears!

JULIET. Romeo!

ROMEO.   My dear!

JULIET.   At what o'clock to-morrow
Shall I send to thee?

ROMEO.   At the hour of nine.

JULIET. I will not fail; 'tis twenty years till then.
I have forgot why I did call thee back.

ROMEO. Let me stand here till thou remember it.

JULIET. I shall forget, to have thee still stand there,
Remembering how I love thy company.

ROMEO. And I'll still stay, to have thee still forget,
Forgetting any other home but this.

JULIET. 'Tis almost morning; I would have thee gone;
And yet no further than a wanton's bird,
Who lets it hop a little from her hand,
Like a poor prisoner in his twisted gyves,
And with a silk thread plucks it back again,
So loving-jealous of his liberty.

ROMEO. I would I were thy bird.

JULIET.   Sweet, so would I:
Yet I should kill thee with much cherishing.
Good-night, good-night! parting is such sweet sorrow
That I shall say good-night till it be morrow.   *Exit*

ROMEO. Sleep dwell upon thine eyes, peace in thy breast!
Would I were sleep and peace, so sweet to rest!
Hence will I to my ghostly father's cell,
His help to crave, and my dear hap to tell.   *Exit*

SCENE THREE

Friar Laurence's Cell.

Enter Friar Laurence, with a basket

FRIAR LAURENCE. The grey-ey'd morn smiles on the frowning night,
Chequering the eastern clouds with streaks of light,
And flecked darkness like a drunkard reels
From forth day's path and Titan's fiery wheels:
Now, ere the sun advance his burning eye
The day to cheer and night's dank dew to dry,
I must up-fill this osier cage of ours
With baleful weeds and precious-juiced flowers.
The earth that's nature's mother is her tomb;
What is her burying grave that is her womb,
And from her womb children of divers kind
We sucking on her natural bosom find,
Many for many virtues excellent,
None but for some, and yet all different.
O! mickle is the powerful grace that lies

In herbs, plants, stones, and their true qualities:
For nought so vile that on the earth doth live
But to the earth some special good doth give,
Nor aught so good but strain'd from that fair use
Revolts from true birth, stumbling on abuse:
Virtue itself turns vice, being misapplied,
And vice sometime's by action dignified.
Within the infant rind of this weak flower
Poison hath residence and medicine power:
For this, being smelt, with that part cheers each part;
Being tasted, slays all senses with the heart.
Two such opposed foes encamp them still
In man as well as herbs, grace and rude will;
And where the worser is predominant,
Full soon the canker death eats up that plant.

Enter Romeo

ROMEO. Good-morrow, father!

FRIAR LAURENCE.   Benedicite!
What early tongue so sweet saluteth me?
Young son, it argues a distemper'd head
So soon to bid good-morrow to thy bed:
Care keeps his watch in every old man's eye,
And where care lodges, sleep will never lie;
But where unbruised youth with unstuff'd brain
Doth couch his limbs, there golden sleep doth reign:
Therefore thy earliness doth me assure
Thou art up-rous'd by some distemperature;
Or if not so, then here I hit it right,
Our Romeo hath not been in bed to-night.

ROMEO. That last is true; the sweeter rest was mine.

FRIAR LAURENCE. God pardon sin! wast thou with Rosaline?

ROMEO. With Rosaline, my ghostly father? no;
I have forgot that name, and that name's woe.

FRIAR LAURENCE. That's my good son: but where hast thou been, then?

ROMEO. I'll tell thee, ere thou ask it me again.
I have been feasting with mine enemy,
Where on a sudden one hath wounded me,
That's by me wounded: both our remedies
Within thy help and holy physics lies:

I bear no hatred, blessed man; for, lo!
My intercession likewise steads my foe.
FRIAR LAURENCE. Be plain, good son, and homely in thy drift;
  Riddling confession finds but riddling shrift.
ROMEO. Then plainly know my heart's dear love is set
  On the fair daughter of rich Capulet:
  As mine on hers, so hers is set on mine;
  And all combin'd, save what thou must combine
  By holy marriage: when and where and how
  We met, we woo'd and made exchange of vow,
  I'll tell thee as we pass; but this I pray,
  That thou consent to marry us to-day.
FRIAR LAURENCE. Holy Saint Francis! what a change is here;
  Is Rosaline, whom thou didst love so dear,
  So soon forsaken? young men's love then lies
  Not truly in their hearts, but in their eyes.
  Jesu Maria! what a deal of brine
  Hath wash'd thy sallow cheeks for Rosaline;
  How much salt water thrown away in waste,
  To season love, that of it doth not taste!
  The sun not yet thy sighs from heaven clears,
  Thy old groans ring yet in my ancient ears;
  Lo! here upon thy cheek the stain doth sit
  Of an old tear that is not wash'd off yet.
  If e'er thou wast thyself and these woes thine,
  Thou and these woes were all for Rosaline:
  And art thou chang'd? pronounce this sentence then:
  Women may fall, when there's no strength in men.
ROMEO. Thou chidd'st me oft for loving Rosaline.
FRIAR LAURENCE. For doting, not for loving, pupil mine.
ROMEO. And bad'st me bury love.
FRIAR LAURENCE.   Not in a grave,
  To lay one in, another out to have.
ROMEO. I pray thee, chide not; she, whom I love now
  Doth grace for grace and love for love allow;
  The other did not so.
FRIAR LAURENCE.   O! she knew well
  Thy love did read by rote and could not spell.
  But come, young waverer, come, go with me,

In one respect I'll thy assistant be;
For this alliance may so happy prove,
To turn your households' rancour to pure love.

ROMEO. O! let us hence; I stand on sudden haste.

FRIAR LAURENCE. Wisely and slow; they stumble that run fast.   *Exeunt*

SCENE FOUR

A Street.

Enter Benvolio and Mercutio

MERCUTIO. Where the devil should this Romeo be?
Came he not home to-night?

BENVOLIO. Not to his father's; I spoke with his man.

MERCUTIO. Why, that same pale hard-hearted wench, that Rosaline,
Torments him so, that he will sure run mad.

BENVOLIO. Tybalt, the kinsman of old Capulet,
Hath sent a letter to his father's house.

MERCUTIO. A challenge, on my life.

BENVOLIO. Romeo will answer it.

MERCUTIO. Any man that can write may answer a letter.

BENVOLIO. Nay, he will answer the letter's master, how he dares, being
dared.

MERCUTIO. Alas! poor Romeo, he is already dead; stabbed with a white
wench's black eye; shot through the ear with a love-song; the very pin
of his heart cleft with the blind bow-boy's butt-shaft; and is he a man
to encounter Tybalt?

BENVOLIO. Why, what is Tybalt?

MERCUTIO. More than prince of cats, I can tell you. O! he is the coura-
geous captain of compliments. He fights as you sing prick-song, keeps
time, distance, and proportion; rests me his minim rest, one, two, and
the third in your bosom; the very butcher of a silk button, a duellist, a
duellist; a gentleman of the very first house, of the first and second
cause. Ah! the immortal passado! the punto reverso! the hay!

BENVOLIO. The what?

MERCUTIO. The pox of such antick, lisping, affecting fantasticoes, these
new tuners of accents!—"By Jesu, a very good blade!—a very tall man!
a very good whore."—Why, is not this a lamentable thing, grandsire, that we should be thus afflicted with these strange flies, these
fashion-mongers, these pardonnez-mois, who stand so much on the

new form that they cannot sit at ease on the old bench? O, their bons, their bons!

Enter Romeo

BENVOLIO. Here comes Romeo, here comes Romeo.

MERCUTIO. Without his roe, like a dried herring. O flesh, flesh, how art thou fishified! Now is he for the numbers that Petrarch flowed in: Laura to his lady was but a kitchen-wench; marry, she had a better love to be-rime her; Dido a dowdy; Cleopatra a gipsy; Helen and Hero hildings and harlots; Thisbe, a grey eye or so, but not to the purpose. Signior Romeo, bon jour! there's a French salutation to your French slop. You gave us the counterfeit fairly last night.

ROMEO. Good-morrow to you both. What counterfeit did I give you?

MERCUTIO. The slip, sir, the slip; can you not conceive?

ROMEO. Pardon, good Mercutio, my business was great; and in such a case as mine a man may strain courtesy.

MERCUTIO. That's as much as to say, such a case as yours constrains a man to bow in the hams.

ROMEO. Meaning—to curtsy.

MERCUTIO. Thou hast most kindly hit it.

ROMEO. A most courteous exposition.

MERCUTIO. Nay, I am the very pink of courtesy.

ROMEO. Pink for flower.

MERCUTIO. Right.

ROMEO. Why, then, is my pump well flowered.

MERCUTIO. Well said; follow me this jest now till thou hast worn out the pump, that, when the single sole of it is worn, the jest may remain after the wearing sole singular.

ROMEO. O single-soled jest! solely singular for the singleness.

MERCUTIO. Come between us, good Benvolio; my wit faints.

ROMEO. Switch and spurs, switch and spurs; or I'll cry a match.

MERCUTIO. Nay, if thy wits run the wild-goose chase, I have done, for thou hast more of the wild-goose in one of thy wits than, I am sure, I have in my whole five. Was I with you there for the goose?

ROMEO. Thou wast never with me for anything when thou wast not here for the goose.

MERCUTIO. I will bite thee by the ear for that jest.

ROMEO. Nay, good goose, bite not.

MERCUTIO. Thy wit is a very bitter sweeting; it is a most sharp sauce.

ROMEO. And is it not then well served in to a sweet goose?

MERCUTIO. O! here's a wit of cheveril, that stretches from an inch narrow to an ell broad.

ROMEO. I stretch it out for that word "broad"; which added to the goose, proves thee far and wide a broad goose.

MERCUTIO. Why, is not this better now than groaning for love? now art thou sociable, now art thou Romeo; now art thou what thou art, by art as well as by nature: for this drivelling love is like a great natural, that runs lolling up and down to hide his bauble in a hole.

BENVOLIO. Stop there, stop there.

MERCUTIO. Thou desirest me to stop in my tale against the hair.

BENVOLIO. Thou wouldst else have made thy tale large.

MERCUTIO. O! thou art deceived; I would have made it short; for I was come to the whole depth of my tale, and meant indeed to occupy the argument no longer.

ROMEO. Here's goodly gear!

Enter Nurse and Peter

MERCUTIO. A sail, a sail!

BENVOLIO. Two, two; a shirt and a smock.

NURSE. Peter!

PETER. Anon!

NURSE. My fan, Peter.

MERCUTIO. Good Peter, to hide her face; for her fan's the fairer face.

NURSE. God ye good morrow, gentlemen.

MERCUTIO. God ye good den, fair gentlewoman.

NURSE. Is it good den?

MERCUTIO. 'Tis no less, I tell you; for the bawdy hand of the dial is now upon the prick of noon.

NURSE. Out upon you! what a man are you!

ROMEO. One, gentlewoman, that God hath made for himself to mar.

NURSE. By my troth, it is well said; "for himself to mar," quoth a'?— Gentlemen, can any of you tell me where I may find the young Romeo?

ROMEO. I can tell you; but young Romeo will be older when you have found him than he was when you sought him: I am the youngest of that name, for fault of a worse.

NURSE. You say well.

MERCUTIO. Yea! is the worst well? very well took, i' faith; wisely, wisely.

NURSE. If you be he, sir, I desire some confidence with you.

BENVOLIO. She will indite him to some supper.

MERCUTIO. A bawd, a bawd, a bawd! So ho!

ROMEO. What hast thou found?

MERCUTIO. No hare, sir; unless a hare, sir, in a lenten pie, that is something stale and hoar ere it spent.   *Sings*

> An old hare hoar, and an old hare hoar,
> > Is very good meat in Lent:
> But a hare that is hoar, is too much for a score,
> > When it hoars ere it be spent.

Romeo, will you come to your father's? we'll to dinner thither.

ROMEO. I will follow you.

MERCUTIO. Farewell, ancient lady; farewell.

> (*Sings*) Lady, lady, lady.

Exeunt Mercutio and Benvolio

NURSE. Marry, farewell! I pray you, sir, what saucy merchant was this, that was so full of his ropery?

ROMEO. A gentleman, nurse, that loves to hear himself talk, and will speak more in a minute than he will stand to in a month.

NURSE. An a' speak anything against me, I'll take him down, an a' were lustier than he is, and twenty such Jacks; and if I cannot, I'll find those that shall. Scurvy knave! I am none of his flirt-gills; I am none of his skeins-mates. (*To Peter*) And thou must stand by too, and suffer every knave to use me at his pleasure!

PETER. I saw no man use you at his pleasure; if I had, my weapon should quickly have been out, I warrant you. I dare draw as soon as another man, if I see occasion in a good quarrel, and the law on my side.

NURSE. Now, afore God, I am so vexed, that every part about me quivers. Scurvy knave! Pray you, sir, a word; and as I told you, my young lady bade me inquire you out; what she bid me say I will keep to myself; but first let me tell ye, if ye should lead her into a fool's paradise, as they say, it were a very gross kind of behaviour, as they say: for the gentlewoman is young; and, therefore, if you should deal double with her, truly it were an ill thing to be offered to any gentlewoman, and very weak dealing.

ROMEO. Nurse, commend me to thy lady and mistress. I protest unto thee,—

NURSE. Good heart! and, i' faith, I will tell her as much. Lord, Lord! she will be a joyful woman.

ROMEO. What wilt thou tell her, nurse? thou dost not mark me.

NURSE. I will tell her, sir, that you do protest; which, as I take it, is a gen-
tlemanlike offer.

ROMEO. Bid her devise
Some means to come to shrift this afternoon;
And there she shall at Friar Laurence' cell
Be shriv'd and married. Here is for thy pains.

NURSE. No, truly, sir; not a penny.

ROMEO. Go to; I say, you shall.

NURSE. This afternoon, sir? well, she shall be there.

ROMEO. And stay, good nurse; behind the abbey wall:
Within this hour my man shall be with thee,
And bring thee cords made like a tackled stair;
Which to the high top-gallant of my joy
Must be my convoy in the secret night.
Farewell! Be trusty, and I'll quit thy pains.
Farewell! Commend me to thy mistress.

NURSE. Now God in heaven bless thee! Hark you, sir.

ROMEO. What sayst thou, my dear nurse?

NURSE. Is your man secret? Did you ne'er hear say,
Two may keep counsel, putting one away?

ROMEO. I warrant thee my man's as true as steel.

NURSE. Well, sir; my mistress is the sweetest lady—Lord, Lord!—when
'twas a little prating thing,—O! there's a nobleman in town, one Paris,
that would fain lay knife aboard; but she, good soul, had as lief see a
toad, a very toad, as see him. I anger her sometimes and tell her that
Paris is the properer man; but, I'll warrant you, when I say so, she looks
as pale as any clout in the versal world. Doth not rosemary and Romeo
begin both with a letter?

ROMEO. Ay, nurse: what of that? both with an R.

NURSE. Ah! mocker; that's the dog's name. R is for the— No; I know it be-
gins with some other letter: and she had the prettiest sententious of it,
of you and rosemary, that it would do you good to hear it.

ROMEO. Commend me to thy lady.

NURSE. Ay, a thousand times. (*Exit Romeo*) Peter!

PETER. Anon!

NURSE. Before, and apace.   *Exeunt*

SCENE FIVE

Capulet's Garden.

Enter Juliet

JULIET. The clock struck nine when I did send the nurse;
In half an hour she promis'd to return.
Perchance she cannot meet him: that's not so.
O! she is lame: love's heralds should be thoughts,
Which ten times faster glide than the sun's beams,
Driving back shadows over lowering hills:
Therefore do nimble-pinion'd doves draw Love,
And therefore hath the wind-swift Cupid wings.
Now is the sun upon the highmost hill
Of this day's journey, and from nine till twelve
Is three long hours, yet she is not come.
Had she affections, and warm youthful blood,
She'd be as swift in motion as a ball;
My words would bandy her to my sweet love,
And his to me:
But old folks, many feign as they were dead;
Unwieldy, slow, heavy and pale as lead.

Enter Nurse and Peter

O God! she comes. O honey nurse! what news?
Hast thou met with him? Send thy man away.

NURSE. Peter, stay at the gate. *Exit Peter*

JULIET. Now, good sweet nurse; O Lord! why look'st thou sad?
Though news be sad, yet tell them merrily;
If good, thou sham'st the music of sweet news
By playing it to me with so sour a face.

NURSE. I am aweary, give me leave awhile:
Fie, how my bones ache! What a jaunce have I had!

JULIET. I would thou hadst my bones, and I thy news.
Nay, come, I pray thee, speak; good, good nurse, speak.

NURSE. Jesu! what haste? can you not stay awhile?
Do you not see that I am out of breath?

JULIET. How art thou out of breath when thou hast breath
To say to me that thou art out of breath?
The excuse that thou dost make in this delay
Is longer than the tale thou dost excuse.

Is thy news good, or bad? answer to that;
Say either, and I'll stay the circumstance:
Let me be satisfied, is 't good or bad?

NURSE. Well, you have made a simple choice; you know not how to
choose a man: Romeo! no, not he; though his face be better than any
man's, yet his leg excels all men's; and for a hand, and a foot, and a
body, though they be not to be talked on, yet they are past compare. He
is not the flower of courtesy, but, I'll warrant him, as gentle as a lamb.
Go thy ways, wench; serve God. What! have you dined at home?

JULIET. No, no: but all this did I know before.
What says he of our marriage? what of that?

NURSE. Lord! how my head aches; what a head have I!
It beats as it would fall in twenty pieces.
My back o' t'other side; O! my back, my back!
Beshrew your heart for sending me about,
To catch my death with jauncing up and down.

JULIET. I' faith, I am sorry that thou art not well.
Sweet, sweet, sweet nurse, tell me, what says my love?

NURSE. Your love says, like an honest gentleman, and a courteous, and a
kind, and a handsome, and, I warrant, a virtuous,—Where is your
mother?

JULIET. Where is my mother! why, she is within;
Where should she be? How oddly thou repliest:
"Your love says, like an honest gentleman,
Where is your mother?"

NURSE.   O! God's lady dear,
Are you so hot? Marry, come up, I trow;
Is this the poultice for my aching bones?
Henceforward do your messages yourself.

JULIET. Here's such a coil! come, what says Romeo?

NURSE. Have you got leave to go to shrift to-day?

JULIET. I have.

NURSE. Then hie you hence to Friar Laurence' cell,
There stays a husband to make you a wife:
Now comes the wanton blood up in your cheeks,
They'll be in scarlet straight at any news.
Hie you to church; I must another way,
To fetch a ladder, by the which your love
Must climb a bird's nest soon when it is dark,

I am the drudge and toil in your delight,
But you shall bear the burden soon at night.
Go; I'll to dinner; hie you to the cell.

JULIET. Hie to high fortune! Honest nurse, farewell.

Exeunt

SCENE SIX

Friar Laurence's Cell.

Enter Friar Laurence and Romeo

FRIAR LAURENCE. So smile the heaven upon this holy act,
That after hours with sorrow chide us not!

ROMEO. Amen, amen! but come what sorrow can,
It cannot countervail the exchange of joy
That one short minute gives me in her sight:
Do thou but close our hands with holy words,
Then love-devouring death do what he dare;
It is enough I may but call her mine.

FRIAR LAURENCE. These violent delights have violent ends,
And in their triumph die, like fire and powder
Which, as they kiss, consume: the sweetest honey
Is loathsome in his own deliciousness
And in the taste confounds the appetite:
Therefore love moderately; long love doth so;
Too swift arrives as tardy as too slow.

Enter Juliet

Here comes the lady: O! so light a foot
Will ne'er wear out the everlasting flint:
A lover may bestride the gossamer
That idles in the wanton summer air,
And yet not fall; so light is vanity.

JULIET. Good-even to my ghostly confessor.

FRIAR LAURENCE. Romeo shall thank thee, daughter, for us both.

JULIET. As much to him, else are his thanks too much.

ROMEO. Ah! Juliet, if the measure of thy joy
Be heap'd like mine, and that thy skill be more
To blazon it, then sweeten with thy breath
This neighbour air, and let rich music's tongue

Unfold the imagin'd happiness that both
Receive in either by this dear encounter.

JULIET. Conceit, more rich in matter than in words.
Brags of his substance, not of ornament:
They are but beggars that can count their worth;
But my true love is grown to such excess
I cannot sum up half my sum of wealth.

FRIAR LAURENCE. Come, come with me, and we will make short work;
For, by your leaves, you shall not stay alone
Till holy church incorporate two in one.   *Exeunt*

ACT THREE

SCENE ONE

Verona. A Public Place.

Enter Mercutio, Benvolio, Page, and Servants

BENVOLIO. I pray thee, good Mercutio, let's retire:
The day is hot, the Capulets abroad,
And, if we meet, we shall not 'scape a brawl;
For now, these hot days, is the mad blood stirring.

MERCUTIO. Thou art like one of those fellows that when he enters the confines of a tavern claps me his sword upon the table, and says "God send me no need of thee!" and by the operation of the second cup draws him on the drawer, when, indeed, there is no need.

BENVOLIO. Am I like such a fellow?

MERCUTIO. Come, come, thou art as hot a Jack in thy mood as any in Italy; and as soon moved to be moody, and as soon moody to be moved.

BENVOLIO. And what to?

MERCUTIO. Nay, an there were two such, we should have none shortly, for one would kill the other. Thou! why, thou wilt quarrel with a man that hath a hair more or a hair less in his beard than thou hast. Thou wilt quarrel with a man for cracking nuts, having no other reason but because thou hast hazel eyes. What eye, but such an eye, would spy out such a quarrel? Thy head is as full of quarrels as an egg is full of meat, and yet thy head hath been beaten as addle as an egg for quarrelling. Thou has quarrelled with a man for coughing in the street, because he hath wakened thy dog that hath lain asleep in the sun. Didst thou not fall out with a tailor for wearing his new doublet before Easter? with another, for tying his new shoes with old riband? and yet thou wilt tutor me from quarrelling!

BENVOLIO. An I were so apt to quarrel as thou art, any man should buy
the fee-simple of my life for an hour and a quarter.
MERCUTIO. The fee-simple! O simple!
BENVOLIO. By my head, here come the Capulets.
MERCUTIO. By my heel, I care not.

Enter Tybalt, and Others

TYBALT. Follow me close, for I will speak to them. Gentlemen, good den!
a word with one of you.
MERCUTIO. And but one word with one of us? Couple it with something;
make it a word and a blow.
TYBALT. You shall find me apt enough to that, sir, an you will give me oc-
casion.
MERCUTIO. Could you not take some occasion without giving?
TYBALT. Mercutio, thou consort'st with Romeo,—
MERCUTIO. Consort! What! dost thou make us minstrels? an thou make
minstrels of us, look to hear nothing but discords: here's my fiddlestick;
here's that shall make you dance. 'Zounds! consort!
BENVOLIO. We talk here in the public haunt of men:
Either withdraw unto some private place,
Or reason coldly of your grievances,
Or else depart; here all eyes gaze on us.
MERCUTIO. Men's eyes were made to look, and let them gaze;
I will not budge for no man's pleasure, I.

Enter Romeo

TYBALT. Well, peace be with you, sir. Here comes my man.
MERCUTIO. But I'll be hang'd, sir, if he wear your livery:
Marry, go before to field, he'll be your follower;
Your worship in that sense may call him "man."
TYBALT. Romeo, the hate I bear thee can afford
No better term than this,—thou art a villain.
ROMEO. Tybalt, the reason that I have to love thee
Doth much excuse the appertaining rage
To such a greeting; villain am I none,
Therefore farewell; I see thou know'st me not.
TYBALT. Boy, this shall not excuse the injuries
That thou hast done me; therefore turn and draw.
ROMEO. I do protest I never injur'd thee,
But love thee better than thou canst devise,
Till thou shalt know the reason of my love:

And so, good Capulet, which name I tender
As dearly as my own, be satisfied.

MERCUTIO. O calm, dishonourable, vile submission!
Alla stoccata carries it away.   *Draws*
Tybalt, you rat-catcher, will you walk?

TYBALT. What wouldst thou have with me?

MERCUTIO. Good king of cats, nothing but one of your nine lives, that I
mean to make bold withal, and, as you shall use me hereafter, dry-beat
the rest of the eight. Will you pluck your sword out of his pilcher by
the ears? make haste, lest mine be about your ears ere it be out.

TYBALT. (*Drawing*) I am for you.

ROMEO. Gentle Mercutio, put thy rapier up.

MERCUTIO. Come, sir, your passado.   *They fight*

ROMEO. Draw, Benvolio; beat down their weapons.
Gentlemen, for shame, forbear this outrage!
Tybalt, Mercutio, the prince expressly hath
Forbidden bandying in Verona streets.
Hold, Tybalt! good Mercutio!   *Exeunt Tybalt and his Partisans*

MERCUTIO.   I am hurt.
A plague o' both your houses! I am sped.
Is he gone, and hath nothing?

BENVOLIO.   What! art thou hurt?

MERCUTIO. Ay, ay, a scratch, a scratch; marry, 'tis enough. Where is my
page? Go, villain, fetch a surgeon.   *Exit Page*

ROMEO. Courage, man; the hurt cannot be much.

MERCUTIO. No, 'tis not so deep as a well, nor so wide as a church door;
but 'tis enough, 'twill serve: ask for me to-morrow, and you shall find
me a grave man. I am peppered, I warrant, for this world. A plague o'
both your houses! Zounds, a dog, a rat, a mouse, a cat, to scratch a man
to death! a braggart, a rogue, a villain, that fights by the book of arith-
metic! Why the devil came you between us? I was hurt under your arm.

ROMEO. I thought all for the best.

MERCUTIO. Help me into some house, Benvolio,
Or I shall faint. A plague o' both your houses!
They have made worms' meat of me: I have it,
And soundly too:—your houses!   *Exeunt Mercutio and Benvolio*

ROMEO. This gentleman, the prince's near ally,
My very friend, hath got his mortal hurt
In my behalf; my reputation stain'd

With Tybalt's slander, Tybalt, that an hour
Hath been my kinsman. O sweet Juliet!
Thy beauty hath made me effeminate,
And in my temper soften'd valour's steel!

Re-enter Benvolio

BENVOLIO. O Romeo, Romeo! brave Mercutio's dead;
    That gallant spirit hath aspir'd the clouds,
    Which too untimely here did scorn the earth.
ROMEO. This day's black fate on more days doth depend;
    This but begins the woe others must end.

Re-enter Tybalt

BENVOLIO. Here comes the furious Tybalt back again.
ROMEO. Alive! in triumph! and Mercutio slain!
    Away to heaven, respective lenity,
    And fire-ey'd fury be my conduct now!
    Now, Tybalt, take the villain back again
    That late thou gav'st me; for Mercutio's soul
    Is but a little way above our heads,
    Staying for thine to keep him company:
    Either thou, or I, or both, must go with him.
TYBALT. Thou wretched boy, that didst consort him here,
    Shalt with him hence.
ROMEO.   This shall determine that.   *They fight: Tybalt falls*
BENVOLIO. Romeo, away! be gone!
    The citizens are up, and Tybalt slain.
    Stand not amaz'd: the prince will doom thee death
    If thou art taken: hence! be gone! away!
ROMEO. O! I am Fortune's fool.
BENVOLIO.   Why dost thou stay?   *Exit Romeo*

Enter Citizens, &c.

FIRST CITIZEN. Which way ran he that kill'd Mercutio?
    Tybalt, that murderer, which way ran he?
BENVOLIO. There lies that Tybalt.
FIRST CITIZEN.   Up, sir, go with me.
    I charge thee in the prince's name, obey.

*Enter Prince, attended; Montague, Capulet,
their Wives, and Others*

PRINCE. Where are the vile beginners of this fray?
BENVOLIO. O noble prince! I can discover all

The unlucky manage of this fatal brawl:
There lies the man, slain by young Romeo,
That slew thy kinsman, brave Mercutio.

LADY CAPULET. Tybalt, my cousin! O my brother's child!
O prince! O cousin! husband! O! the blood is spill'd
Of my dear kinsman. Prince, as thou art true,
For blood of ours shed blood of Montague.
O cousin, cousin!

PRINCE. Benvolio, who began this bloody fray?

BENVOLIO. Tybalt, here slain, whom Romeo's hand did slay:
Romeo, that spoke him fair, bade him bethink
How nice the quarrel was, and urg'd withal
Your high displeasure: all this, uttered
With gentle breath, calm look, knees humbly bow'd,
Could not take truce with the unruly spleen
Of Tybalt deaf to peace, but that he tilts
With piercing steel at bold Mercutio's breast,
Who, all as hot, turns deadly point to point,
And, with a martial scorn, with one hand beats
Cold death aside, and with the other sends
It back to Tybalt, whose dexterity
Retorts it: Romeo he cries aloud,
"Hold, friends! friends, part!" and, swifter than his tongue,
His agile arm beats down their fatal points,
And 'twixt them rushes; underneath whose arm
An envious thrust from Tybalt hit the life
Of stout Mercutio, and then Tybalt fled;
But by and by comes back to Romeo,
Who had but newly entertain'd revenge,
And to 't they go like lightning, for, ere I
Could draw to part them, was stout Tybalt slain,
And, as he fell, did Romeo turn and fly.
This is the truth, or let Benvolio die.

LADY CAPULET. He is a kinsman to the Montague;
Affection makes him false, he speaks not true:
Some twenty of them fought in this black strife
And all those twenty could but kill one life.
I beg for justice, which thou, prince, must give;
Romeo slew Tybalt, Romeo must not live.

PRINCE. Romeo slew him, he slew Mercutio;
    Who now the price of his dear blood doth owe?
MONTAGUE. Not Romeo, prince, he was Mercutio's friend,
    His fault concludes but what the law should end,
    The life of Tybalt.
PRINCE.   And for that offence
    Immediately we do exile him hence:
    I have an interest in your hate's proceeding,
    My blood for your rude brawls doth lie a-bleeding;
    But I'll amerce you with so strong a fine
    That you shall all repent the loss of mine.
    I will be deaf to pleading and excuses;
    Nor tears nor prayers shall purchase out abuses;
    Therefore use none; let Romeo hence in haste,
    Else, when he's found, that hour is his last.
    Bear hence this body and attend our will:
    Mercy but murders, pardoning those that kill.   *Exeunt*

SCENE TWO

Capulet's Orchard.

Enter Juliet

JULIET. Gallop apace, you fiery-footed steeds,
    Towards Phoebus' lodging; such a waggoner
    As Phaethon would whip you to the west,
    And bring in cloudy night immediately.
    Spread thy close curtain, love-performing night!
    That runaway's eyes may wink, and Romeo
    Leap to these arms, untalk'd of and unseen!
    Lovers can see to do their amorous rites
    By their own beauties; or, if love be blind,
    It best agrees with night. Come, civil night,
    Thou sober-suited matron, all in black,
    And learn me how to lose a winning match,
    Play'd for a pair of stainless maidenhoods:
    Hood my unmann'd blood, bating in my cheeks,
    With thy black mantle; till strange love, grown bold,
    Think true love acted simple modesty.
    Come, night! come, Romeo! come, thou day in night!

For thou wilt lie upon the wings of night,
Whiter than new snow on a raven's back.
Come, gentle night; come, loving, black-brow'd night,
Give me my Romeo: and, when he shall die,
Take him and cut him out in little stars,
And he will make the face of heaven so fine
That all the world will be in love with night,
And pay no worship to the garish sun.
O! I have bought the mansion of a love,
But not possess'd it, and, though I am sold,
Not yet enjoy'd. So tedious is this day
As is the night before some festival
To an impatient child that hath new robes
And may not wear them. O! here comes my nurse,

Enter Nurse with cords

And she brings news; and every tongue that speaks
But Romeo's name speaks heavenly eloquence.
Now, nurse, what news? What hast thou there? the cords
That Romeo bade thee fetch?

NURSE.   Ay, ay, the cords.   *Throws them down*
JULIET. Ah me! what news? why dost thou wring thy hands?
NURSE. Ah well-a-day! he's dead, he's dead, he's dead!
We are undone, lady, we are undone!
Alack the day! he's gone, he's kill'd, he's dead!
JULIET. Can heaven be so envious?
NURSE.   Romeo can,
Though heaven cannot. O! Romeo, Romeo;
Who ever would have thought it? Romeo!
JULIET. What devil art thou that dost torment me thus?
This torture should be roar'd in dismal hell.
Hath Romeo slain himself? say thou but "I,"
And that bare vowel, "I," shall poison more
Than the death-darting eye of cockatrice:
I am not I, if there be such an "I";
Or those eyes shut that make thee answer "I."
If he be slain, say "I"; or if not, "no":
Brief sounds determine of my weal or woe.
NURSE. I saw the wound, I saw it with mine eyes,
God save the mark! here on his manly breast:

A piteous corse, a bloody piteous corse;
Pale, pale as ashes, all bedaub'd in blood,
All in gore blood; I swounded at the sight.

JULIET. O break, my heart!—poor bankrupt, break at once!
To prison, eyes, ne'er look on liberty!
Vile earth, to earth resign; end motion here;
And thou and Romeo press one heavy bier!

NURSE. O Tybalt, Tybalt! the best friend I had:
O courteous Tybalt! honest gentleman!
That ever I should live to see thee dead!

JULIET. What storm is this that blows so contrary?
Is Romeo slaughter'd, and is Tybalt dead?
My dearest cousin, and my dearer lord?
Then, dreadful trumpet, sound the general doom!
For who is living if those two are gone?

NURSE. Tybalt is gone, and Romeo banished;
Romeo, that kill'd him, he is banished.

JULIET. O God! did Romeo's hand shed Tybalt's blood?

NURSE. It did, it did; alas the day! it did.

JULIET. O serpent heart, hid with a flowering face!
Did ever dragon keep so fair a cave?
Beautiful tyrant! fiend angelical!
Dove-feather'd raven! wolvish-ravening lamb!
Despised substance of divinest show!
Just opposite to what thou justly seem'st;
A damned saint, an honourable villain!
O, nature! what hadst thou to do in hell
When thou didst bower the spirit of a fiend
In mortal paradise of such sweet flesh?
Was ever book containing such vile matter
So fairly bound? O! that deceit should dwell
In such a gorgeous palace.

NURSE.   There's no trust,
No faith, no honesty in men; all naught,
All perjur'd, all dissemblers, all forsworn.
Ah! where's my man? give me some aqua vitæ:
These griefs, these woes, these sorrows make me old.
Shame come to Romeo!

JULIET.   Blister'd be thy tongue

For such a wish! he was not born to shame:
Upon his brow shame is asham'd to sit;
For 'tis a throne where honour may be crown'd
Sole monarch of the universal earth.
O! what a beast was I to chide at him.
NURSE. Will you speak well of him that kill'd your cousin?
JULIET. Shall I speak ill of him that is my husband?
Ah! poor my lord, what tongue shall smooth thy name,
When I, thy three-hours wife, have mangled it?
But, wherefore, villain, didst thou kill my cousin?
That villain cousin would have kill'd my husband:
Back, foolish tears, back to your native spring;
Your tributary drops belong to woe,
Which you, mistaking, offer up to joy.
My husband lives, that Tybalt would have slain;
And Tybalt's dead, that would have slain my husband:
All this is comfort; wherefore weep I then?
Some word there was, worser than Tybalt's death,
That murder'd me: I would forget it fain;
But O! it presses to my memory,
Like damned guilty deeds to sinners' minds.
"Tybalt is dead, and Romeo banished"!
That "banished," that one word "banished,"
Hath slain ten thousand Tybalts. Tybalt's death
Was woe enough, if it had ended there:
Or, if sour woe delights in fellowship,
And needly will be rank'd with other griefs,
Why follow'd not, when she said "Tybalt's dead,"
Thy father, or thy mother, nay, or both,
Which modern lamentation might have mov'd?
But with a rearward following Tybalt's death,
"Romeo is banished"! to speak that word
Is father, mother, Tybalt, Romeo, Juliet,
All slain, all dead: "Romeo is banished"!
There is no end, no limit, measure, bound
In that word's death; no words can that woe sound.—
Where is my father and my mother, nurse?
NURSE. Weeping and wailing over Tybalt's corse:
Will you go to them? I will bring you thither.

JULIET. Wash they his wounds with tears: mine shall be spent,
    When theirs are dry, for Romeo's banishment.
    Take up those cords. Poor ropes, you are beguil'd,
    Both you and I, for Romeo is exil'd:
    He made you for a highway to my bed,
    But I, a maid, die maiden-widowed.
    Come, cords; come, nurse; I'll to my wedding-bed;
    And death, not Romeo, take my maidenhead!
NURSE. Hie to your chamber; I'll find Romeo
    To comfort you: I wot well where he is.
    Hark ye, your Romeo will be here to-night:
    I'll to him; he is hid at Laurence' cell.
JULIET. O! find him; give this ring to my true knight,
    And bid him come to take his last farewell.   *Exeunt*

SCENE THREE

Friar Laurence's Cell.

Enter Friar Laurence

FRIAR LAURENCE. Romeo, come forth; come forth, thou fearful man:
    Affliction is enamour'd of thy parts,
    And thou art wedded to calamity.

Enter Romeo

ROMEO. Father, what news? what is the prince's doom?
    What sorrow craves acquaintance at my hand,
    That I yet know not?
FRIAR LAURENCE. Too familiar
    Is my dear son with such sour company:
    I bring thee tidings of the prince's doom.
ROMEO. What less than doomsday is the prince's doom?
FRIAR LAURENCE. A gentler judgment vanish'd from his lips,
    Not body's death, but body's banishment.
ROMEO. Ha! banishment! be merciful, say "death";
    For exile hath more terror in his look,
    Much more than death: do not say "banishment."
FRIAR LAURENCE. Hence from Verona art thou banished.
    Be patient, for the world is broad and wide.
ROMEO. There is no world without Verona walls,
    But purgatory, torture, hell itself.

Hence banished is banish'd from the world,
And world's exile is death; then "banished,"
Is death mis-term'd. Calling death "banished,"
Thou cutt'st my head off with a golden axe,
And smil'st upon the stroke that murders me.
FRIAR LAURENCE. O deadly sin! O rude unthankfulness!
Thy fault our law calls death; but the kind prince,
Taking thy part, hath rush'd aside the law,
And turn'd that black word death to banishment:
This is dear mercy, and thou seest it not.
ROMEO. 'Tis torture, and not mercy: heaven is here,
Where Juliet lives; and every cat and dog
And little mouse, every unworthy thing,
Live here in heaven and may look on her;
But Romeo may not: more validity,
More honourable state, more courtship lives
In carrion flies than Romeo: they may seize
On the white wonder of dear Juliet's hand,
And steal immortal blessing from her lips,
Who, even in pure and vestal modesty,
Still blush, as thinking their own kisses sin;
Flies may do this, but I from this must fly:
They are free men, but I am banished.
And sayst thou yet that exile is not death?
Hadst thou no poison mix'd, no sharp-ground knife,
No sudden mean of death, though ne'er so mean,
But "banished" to kill me? "Banished"!
O friar! the damned use that word in hell;
Howlings attend it: how hast thou the heart,
Being a divine, a ghostly confessor,
A sin-absolver, and my friend profess'd,
To mangle me with that word "banished"?
FRIAR LAURENCE. Thou fond mad man, hear me but speak a word.
ROMEO. O! thou wilt speak again of banishment.
FRIAR LAURENCE. I'll give thee armour to keep off that word;
Adversity's sweet milk, philosophy,
To comfort thee, though thou art banished.
ROMEO. Yet "banished"! Hang up philosophy.
Unless philosophy can make a Juliet,

Displant a town, reverse a prince's doom,
It helps not, it prevails not: talk no more.
FRIAR LAURENCE. O! then I see that madmen have no ears.
ROMEO. How should they, when that wise men have no eyes?
FRIAR LAURENCE. Let me dispute with thee of thy estate.
ROMEO. Thou canst not speak of that thou dost not feel:
Wert thou as young as I, Juliet thy love,
An hour but married, Tybalt murdered,
Doting like me, and like me banished,
Then mightst thou speak, then mightst thou tear thy hair,
And fall upon the ground, as I do now,
Taking the measure of an unmade grave.   *Knocking within*
FRIAR LAURENCE. Arise; one knocks: good Romeo, hide thyself.
ROMEO. Not I; unless the breath of heart-sick groans,
Mist-like, infold me from the search of eyes.   *Knocking*
FRIAR LAURENCE. Hark! how they knock. Who's there?
Romeo, arise;
Thou wilt be taken. Stay awhile! Stand up;   *Knocking*
Run to my study. By and by! God's will!
What wilfulness is this! I come, I come!   *Knocking*
Who knocks so hard? whence come you? what's your will?
NURSE. (*Within*) Let me come in, and you shall know my errand:
I come from Lady Juliet.
FRIAR LAURENCE.   Welcome, then.
                        Enter Nurse
NURSE. O holy friar! O! tell me, holy friar,
Where is my lady's lord? where's Romeo?
FRIAR LAURENCE. There on the ground, with his own tears made drunk.
NURSE. O! he is even in my mistress' case,
Just in her case!
FRIAR LAURENCE. O woeful sympathy!
Piteous predicament! Even so lies she,
Blubbering and weeping, weeping and blubbering.
Stand up, stand up; stand, an you be a man:
For Juliet's sake, for her sake, rise and stand;
Why should you fall into so deep an O?
ROMEO. Nurse!
NURSE. Ah, sir! ah, sir! Well, death's the end of all.
ROMEO. Spak'st thou of Juliet? how is it with her?

Doth she not think me an old murderer,
Now I have stain'd the childhood of our joy
With blood remov'd but little from her own?
Where is she? and how doth she? and what says
My conceal'd lady to our cancell'd love?

NURSE. O! she says nothing, sir, but weeps and weeps;
And now falls on her bed; and then starts up,
And Tybalt calls, and then on Romeo cries,
And then down falls again.

ROMEO.   As if that name,
Shot from the deadly level of a gun,
Did murder her; as that name's cursed hand
Murder'd her kinsman. O! tell me, friar, tell me,
In what vile part of this anatomy
Doth my name lodge? tell me, that I may sack
The hateful mansion.   *Drawing his sword*

FRIAR LAURENCE.   Hold thy desperate hand:
Art thou a man? thy form cries out thou art:
Thy tears are womanish; thy wild acts denote
The unreasonable fury of a beast:
Unseemly woman in a seeming man;
Or ill-beseeming beast in seeming both!
Thou hast amaz'd me: by my holy order,
I thought thy disposition better temper'd.
Hast thou slain Tybalt? wilt thou slay thyself?
And slay thy lady that in thy life lives,
By doing damned hate upon thyself?
Why rail'st thou on thy birth, the heaven, and earth?
Since birth, and heaven, and earth, all three do meet
In thee at once, which thou at once wouldst lose.
Fie, fie! thou sham'st thy shape, thy love, thy wit,
Which, like a usurer, abound'st in all,
And usest none in that true use indeed
Which should bedeck thy shape, thy love, thy wit.
Thy noble shape is but a form of wax,
Digressing from the valour of a man;
Thy dear love, sworn, but hollow perjury,
Killing that love which thou hast vow'd to cherish;
Thy wit, that ornament to shape and love,

Misshapen in the conduct of them both,
Like powder in a skilless soldier's flask,
To set a-fire by thine own ignorance,
And thou dismember'd with thine own defence.
What! rouse thee, man; thy Juliet is alive,
For whose dear sake thou wast but lately dead;
There art thou happy: Tybalt would kill thee,
But thou slew'st Tybalt; there art thou happy too:
The law that threaten'd death becomes thy friend,
And turns it to exile; there art thou happy:
A pack of blessings light upon thy back;
Happiness courts thee in her best array;
But, like a misbehav'd and sullen wench,
Thou pout'st upon thy fortune and thy love.
Take heed, take heed, for such die miserable.
Go, get thee to thy love, as was decreed,
Ascend her chamber, hence and comfort her;
But look thou stay not till the watch be set,
For then thou canst not pass to Mantua;
Where thou shalt live, till we can find a time
To blaze your marriage, reconcile your friends,
Beg pardon of the prince, and call thee back
With twenty hundred thousand times more joy
Than thou went'st forth in lamentation.
Go before, nurse: commend me to thy lady;
And bid her hasten all the house to bed,
Which heavy sorrow makes them apt unto:
Romeo is coming.

NURSE. O Lord! I could have stay'd here all the night
To hear good counsel: O! what learning is.
My lord, I'll tell my lady you will come.

ROMEO. Do so, and bid my sweet prepare to chide.

NURSE. Here, sir, a ring she bid me give you, sir.
Hie you, make haste, for it grows very late.   *Exit*

ROMEO. How well my comfort is reviv'd by this!

FRIAR LAURENCE. Go hence; good-night; and here stands all your state:
Either be gone before the watch be set,
Or by the break of day disguis'd from hence:
Sojourn in Mantua; I'll find out your man,

And he shall signify from time to time
Every good hap to you that chances here.
Give me thy hand; 'tis late: farewell; good-night.
ROMEO. But that a joy past joy calls out on me,
It were a grief so brief to part with thee:
Farewell.   *Exeunt*

SCENE FOUR

A Room in Capulet's House.

Enter Capulet, Lady Capulet, and Paris

CAPULET. Things have fall'n out, sir, so unluckily,
That we have had no time to move our daughter:
Look you, she lov'd her kinsman Tybalt dearly,
And so did I: well, we were born to die.
'Tis very late, she'll not come down to-night:
I promise you, but for your company,
I would have been a-bed an hour ago.
PARIS. These times of woe afford no time to woo.
Madam, good-night: commend me to your daughter.
LADY CAPULET. I will, and know her mind, early to-morrow;
To-night she's mew'd up to her heaviness.
CAPULET. Sir Paris, I will make a desperate tender
Of my child's love: I think she will be rul'd
In all respects by me; nay, more, I doubt it not.
Wife, go you to her ere you go to bed;
Acquaint her here of my son Paris' love;
And bid her, mark you me, on Wednesday next—
But, soft! what day is this?
PARIS.   Monday, my lord.
CAPULET. Monday! ha, ha! Well, Wednesday is too soon;
O' Thursday let it be: o' Thursday, tell her,
She shall be married to this noble earl.
Will you be ready? do you like this haste?
We'll keep no great ado; a friend or two;
For, hark you, Tybalt being slain so late,
It may be thought we held him carelessly,
Being our kinsman, if we revel much.
Therefore we'll have some half a dozen friends,
And there an end. But what say you to Thursday?

PARIS. My lord, I would that Thursday were to-morrow.

CAPULET. Well, get you gone: o' Thursday be it then.

    Go you to Juliet ere you go to bed,

    Prepare her, wife, against this wedding-day.

    Farewell, my lord. Light to my chamber, ho!

    Afore me! it is so very very late,

    That we may call it early by and by.

    Good-night.   *Exeunt*

SCENE FIVE

Capulet's Orchard.

Enter Romeo and Juliet, above, at the window

JULIET. Wilt thou be gone? it is not yet near day.

    It was the nightingale, and not the lark,

    That pierc'd the fearful hollow of thine ear;

    Nightly she sings on yon pomegranate-tree:

    Believe me, love, it was the nightingale.

ROMEO. It was the lark, the herald of the morn,

    No nightingale: look, love, what envious streaks

    Do lace the severing clouds in yonder east:

    Night's candles are burnt out, and jocund day

    Stands tiptoe on the misty mountain tops:

    I must be gone and live, or stay and die.

JULIET. Yon light is not daylight, I know it, I:

    It is some meteor that the sun exhales,

    To be to thee this night a torch-bearer,

    And light thee on thy way to Mantua:

    Therefore stay yet; thou need'st not be gone.

ROMEO. Let me be ta'en, let me be put to death;

    I am content, so thou wilt have it so.

    I'll say yon grey is not the morning's eye,

    'Tis but the pale reflex of Cynthia's brow;

    Nor that is not the lark, whose notes do beat

    The vaulty heaven so high above our heads:

    I have more care to stay than will to go:

    Come, death, and welcome! Juliet wills it so.

    How is 't, my soul? let's talk; it is not day.

JULIET. It is, it is; hie hence, be gone, away!

It is the lark that sings so out of tune,
Straining harsh discords and unpleasing sharps.
Some say the lark makes sweet division;
This doth not so, for she divideth us:
Some say the lark and loathed toad change eyes;
O! now I would they had chang'd voices too,
Since arm from arm that voice doth us affray,
Hunting thee hence with hunts-up to the day.
O! now be gone; more light and light it grows.

ROMEO. More light and light; more dark and dark our woes.

Enter Nurse

NURSE. Madam!

JULIET. Nurse!

NURSE. Your lady mother is coming to your chamber:
The day is broke; be wary, look about.   *Exit*

JULIET. Then, window, let day in, and let life out.

ROMEO. Farewell, farewell! one kiss, and I'll descend.   *Descends*

JULIET. Art thou gone so? my lord, my love, my friend!
I must hear from thee every day in the hour,
For in a minute there are many days:
O! by this count I shall be much in years
Ere I again behold my Romeo.

ROMEO. Farewell!
I will omit no opportunity
That may convey my greetings, love, to thee.

JULIET. O! think'st thou we shall ever meet again?

ROMEO. I doubt it not; and all these woes shall serve
For sweet discourses in our time to come.

JULIET. O God! I have an ill-divining soul:
Methinks I see thee, now thou art so low,
As one dead in the bottom of a tomb:
Either my eyesight fails, or thou look'st pale.

ROMEO. And trust me, love, in my eye so do you:
Dry sorrow drinks our blood. Adieu! adieu!   *Exit*

JULIET. O fortune, fortune! all men call thee fickle:
If thou art fickle, what dost thou with him
That is renown'd for faith? Be fickle, fortune;
For then, I hope, thou wilt not keep him long,
But send him back.

LADY CAPULET. (*Within*) Ho, daughter! are you up?
JULIET. Who is 't that calls? is it my lady mother?
  Is she not down so late, or up so early?
  What unaccustom'd cause procures her hither?
                    Enter Lady Capulet
LADY CAPULET. Why, how now, Juliet!
JULIET.   Madam, I am not well.
LADY CAPULET. Evermore weeping for your cousin's death?
  What! wilt thou wash him from his grave with tears?
  And if thou couldst, thou couldst not make him live;
  Therefore, have done: some grief shows much of love;
  But much of grief shows still some want of wit.
JULIET. Yet let me weep for such a feeling loss.
LADY CAPULET. So shall you feel the loss, but not the friend
  Which you weep for.
JULIET.   Feeling so the loss,
  I cannot choose but ever weep the friend.
LADY CAPULET. Well, girl, thou weep'st not so much for his death,
  As that the villain lives which slaughter'd him.
JULIET. What villain, madam?
LADY CAPULET.   That same villain, Romeo.
JULIET. (*Aside*) Villain and he be many miles asunder.
  God pardon him! I do, with all my heart;
  And yet no man like he doth grieve my heart.
LADY CAPULET. That is because the traitor murderer lives.
JULIET. Ay, madam, from the reach of these my hands.
  Would none but I might venge my cousin's death!
LADY CAPULET. We will have vengeance for it, fear thou not:
  Then weep no more. I'll send to one in Mantua,
  Where that same banish'd runagate doth live,
  Shall give him such an unaccustom'd dram
  That he shall soon keep Tybalt company:
  And then, I hope, thou wilt be satisfied.
JULIET. Indeed, I never shall be satisfied
  With Romeo, till I behold him—dead—
  Is my poor heart so for a kinsman vex'd:
  Madam, if you could find out but a man
  To bear a poison, I would temper it,
  That Romeo should, upon receipt thereof,

Soon sleep in quiet. O! how my heart abhors
To hear him nam'd, and cannot come to him,
To wreak the love I bore my cousin Tybalt
Upon his body that hath slaughter'd him.
LADY CAPULET. Find thou the means, and I'll find such a man.
But now I'll tell thee joyful tidings, girl.
JULIET. And joy comes well in such a needy time:
What are they, I beseech your ladyship?
LADY CAPULET. Well, well, thou hast a careful father, child;
One who, to put thee from thy heaviness,
Hath sorted out a sudden day of joy
That thou expect'st not, nor I look'd not for.
JULIET. Madam, in happy time, what day is that?
LADY CAPULET. Marry, my child, early next Thursday morn
The gallant, young, and noble gentleman,
The County Paris, at Saint Peter's church,
Shall happily make thee there a joyful bride.
JULIET. Now, by Saint Peter's church, and Peter too,
He shall not make me there a joyful bride.
I wonder at this haste; that I must wed
Ere he that should be husband comes to woo.
I pray you, tell my lord and father, madam,
I will not marry yet; and, when I do, I swear,
It shall be Romeo, whom you know I hate,
Rather than Paris. These are news indeed!
LADY CAPULET. Here comes your father; tell him so yourself,
And see how he will take it at your hands.

Enter Capulet and Nurse

CAPULET. When the sun sets, the air doth drizzle dew;
But for the sunset of my brother's son
It rains downright.
How now! a conduit, girl? what! still in tears?
Evermore showering? In one little body
Thou counterfeit'st a bark, a sea, a wind;
For still thy eyes, which I may call the sea,
Do ebb and flow with tears; the bark thy body is,
Sailing in this salt flood; the winds, thy sighs;
Who, raging with thy tears, and they with them,
Without a sudden calm, will overset

Thy tempest-tossed body. How now, wife!
Have you deliver'd to her our decree?
LADY CAPULET. Ay, sir; but she will none, she gives you thanks.
I would the fool were married to her grave!
CAPULET. Soft! take me with you, take me with you, wife.
How! will she none? doth she not give us thanks?
Is she not proud? doth she not count her bless'd,
Unworthy as she is, that we have wrought
So worthy a gentleman to be her bridegroom?
JULIET. Not proud, you have; but thankful, that you have:
Proud can I never be of what I hate;
But thankful even for hate, that is meant love.
CAPULET. How now! how now, chop-logic! What is this?
"Proud," and "I thank you," and "I thank you not";
And yet "not proud"; mistress minion, you,
Thank me no thankings, nor proud me no prouds,
But fettle your fine joints 'gainst Thursday next,
To go with Paris to Saint Peter's church,
Or I will drag thee on a hurdle thither.
Out, you green-sickness carrion! out, you baggage!
You tallow face!
LADY CAPULET. Fie, fie! what, are you mad?
JULIET. Good father, I beseech you on my knees,
Hear me with patience but to speak a word.
CAPULET. Hang thee, young baggage! disobedient wretch!
I tell thee what, get thee to church o' Thursday,
Or never after look me in the face,
Speak not, reply not, do not answer me;
My fingers itch.—Wife, we scarce thought us bless'd
That God had lent us but this only child;
But now I see this one is one too much,
And that we have a curse in having her.
Out on her, hilding!
NURSE.   God in heaven bless her!
You are to blame, my lord, to rate her so.
CAPULET. And why, my lady wisdom? hold your tongue,
Good prudence; smatter with your gossips, go.
NURSE. I speak no treason.
CAPULET.   O! God ye good den.

NURSE. May not one speak?

CAPULET.   Peace, you mumbling fool;
  Utter your gravity o'er a gossip's bowl;
  For here we need it not.

LADY CAPULET.   You are too hot.

CAPULET. God's bread! it makes me mad.
  Day, night, hour, tide, time, work, play,
  Alone, in company, still my care hath been
  To have her match'd; and having now provided
  A gentleman of noble parentage,
  Of fair demesnes, youthful, and nobly train'd,
  Stuff'd, as they say, with honourable parts,
  Proportion'd as one's thought would wish a man!
  And then to have a wretched puling fool,
  A whining mammet, in her fortune's tender,
  To answer "I'll not wed," "I cannot love,"
  "I am too young," "I pray you, pardon me";
  But, an you will not wed, I'll pardon you:
  Graze where you will, you shall not house with me:
  Look to 't, think on 't, I do not use to jest.
  Thursday is near; lay hand on heart, advise.
  An you be mine, I'll give you to my friend;
  An you be not, hang, beg, starve, die in the streets,
  For, by my soul, I'll ne'er acknowledge thee,
  Nor what is mine shall never do thee good.
  Trust to 't, bethink you; I'll not be forsworn.   *Exit*

JULIET. Is there no pity sitting in the clouds,
  That sees into the bottom of my grief?
  O! sweet my mother, cast me not away:
  Delay this marriage for a month, a week;
  Or, if you do not, make the bridal bed
  In that dim monument where Tybalt lies.

LADY CAPULET. Talk not to me, for I'll not speak a word.
  Do as thou wilt, for I have done with thee.   *Exit*

JULIET. O God!—O nurse! how shall this be prevented?
  My husband is on earth, my faith in heaven;
  How shall that faith return again to earth,
  Unless that husband send it me from heaven
  By leaving earth? comfort me, counsel me.

    Alack, alack! that heaven should practise stratagems
    Upon so soft a subject as myself!
    What sayst thou? hast thou not a word of joy?
    Some comfort, nurse?
NURSE.   Faith, here it is. Romeo
    Is banished; and all the world to nothing
    That he dares ne'er come back to challenge you;
    Or, if he do, it needs must be by stealth.
    Then, since the case so stands as now it doth,
    I think it best you married with the county.
    O! he's a lovely gentleman;
    Romeo's a dishclout to him: an eagle, madam,
    Hath not so green, so quick, so fair an eye
    As Paris hath. Beshrew my very heart,
    I think you are happy in this second match,
    For it excels your first: or if it did not,
    Your first is dead; or 'twere as good he were,
    As living here and you no use of him.
JULIET. Speakest thou from thy heart?
NURSE.   And from my soul too;
    Or else beshrew them both.
JULIET.   Amen!
NURSE.   What!
JULIET. Well, thou hast comforted me marvellous much.
    Go in; and tell my lady I am gone,
    Having displeas'd my father, to Laurence' cell,
    To make confession and to be absolv'd.
NURSE. Marry, I will; and this is wisely done.   *Exit*
JULIET. Ancient damnation! O most wicked fiend!
    Is it more sin to wish me thus forsworn,
    Or to dispraise my lord with that same tongue
    Which she hath prais'd him with above compare
    So many thousand times? Go, counsellor;
    Thou and my bosom henceforth shall be twain.
    I'll to the friar, to know his remedy:
    If all else fail, myself have power to die.   *Exit*

ACT FOUR

SCENE ONE

Verona. Friar Laurence's Cell.

Enter Friar Laurence and Paris

FRIAR LAURENCE. On Thursday, sir? the time is very short.

PARIS. My father Capulet will have it so;
   And I am nothing slow to slack his haste.

FRIAR LAURENCE. You say you do not know the lady's mind:
   Uneven is the course, I like it not.

PARIS. Immoderately she weeps for Tybalt's death,
   And therefore have I little talk'd of love;
   For Venus smiles not in a house of tears.
   Now, sir, her father counts it dangerous
   That she doth give her sorrow so much sway,
   And in his wisdom hastes our marriage
   To stop the inundation of her tears;
   Which, too much minded by herself alone,
   May be put from her by society.
   Now do you know the reason of this haste.

FRIAR LAURENCE. (*Aside*) I would I knew not why it should be slow'd.
   Look, sir, here comes the lady towards my cell.

Enter Juliet

PARIS. Happily met, my lady and my wife!

JULIET. That may be, sir, when I may be a wife.

PARIS. That may be must be, love, on Thursday next.

JULIET. What must be shall be.

FRIAR LAURENCE.   That's a certain text.

PARIS. Come you to make confession to this father?

JULIET. To answer that, I should confess to you.

PARIS. Do not deny to him that you love me.

JULIET. I will confess to you that I love him.

PARIS. So will ye, I am sure, that you love me.

JULIET. If I do so, it will be of more price,
  Being spoke behind your back, than to your face.

PARIS. Poor soul, thy face is much abus'd with tears.

JULIET. The tears have got small victory by that;
  For it was bad enough before their spite.

PARIS. Thou wrong'st it, more than tears, with that report.

JULIET. That is no slander, sir, which is a truth;
  And what I spake, I spake it to my face.

PARIS. Thy face is mine, and thou hast slander'd it.

JULIET. It may be so, for it is not mine own.
  Are you at leisure, holy father, now;
  Or shall I come to you at evening mass?

FRIAR LAURENCE. My leisure serves me, pensive daughter, now:
  My lord, we must entreat the time alone.

PARIS. God shield I should disturb devotion!
  Juliet, on Thursday early will I rouse you:
  Till then, adieu: and keep this holy kiss.   *Exit*

JULIET. O! shut the door! and when thou hast done so,
  Come weep with me; past hope, past cure, past help!

FRIAR LAURENCE. Ah! Juliet, I already know thy grief;
  It strains me past the compass of my wits:
  I hear thou must, and nothing may prorogue it,
  On Thursday next be married to this county.

JULIET. Tell me not, friar, that thou hear'st of this,
  Unless thou tell me how I may prevent it:
  If, in thy wisdom, thou canst give no help,
  Do thou but call my resolution wise,
  And with this knife, I'll help it presently.
  God join'd my heart and Romeo's, thou our hands;
  And ere this hand, by thee to Romeo seal'd,
  Shall be the label to another deed,
  Or my true heart with treacherous revolt
  Turn to another, this shall slay them both.
  Therefore, out of thy long-experienc'd time,
  Give me some present counsel; or behold,

'Twixt my extremes and me this bloody knife
Shall play the umpire, arbitrating that
Which the commission of thy years and art
Could to no issue of true honour bring.
Be not so long to speak; I long to die,
If what thou speak'st speak not of remedy.

FRIAR LAURENCE. Hold, daughter; I do spy a kind of hope,
Which craves as desperate an execution
As that is desperate which we would prevent.
If, rather than to marry County Paris,
Thou hast the strength of will to slay thyself,
Then is it likely thou wilt undertake
A thing like death to chide away this shame,
That cop'st with death himself to 'scape from it;
And, if thou dar'st, I'll give thee remedy.

JULIET. O! bid me leap, rather than marry Paris,
From off the battlements of yonder tower;
Or walk in thievish ways; or bid me lurk
Where serpents are; chain me with roaring bears;
Or shut me nightly in a charnel-house,
O'er-cover'd quite with dead men's rattling bones,
With reeky shanks, and yellow chapless skulls;
Or bid me go into a new-made grave
And hide me with a dead man in his shroud;
Things that, to hear them told, have made me tremble;
And I will do it without fear or doubt,
To live an unstain'd wife to my sweet love.

FRIAR LAURENCE. Hold, then; go home, be merry, give consent
To marry Paris: Wednesday is to-morrow:
To-morrow night look that thou lie alone,
Let not thy nurse lie with thee in thy chamber:
Take thou this vial, being then in bed,
And this distilled liquor drink thou off;
When presently through all thy veins shall run
A cold and drowsy humour, for no pulse
Shall keep his native progress, but surcease;
No warmth, no breath, shall testify, thou liv'st;
The roses in thy lips and cheeks shall fade
To paly ashes; thy eyes' windows fall,

Like death, when he shuts up the day of life;
Each part, depriv'd of supple government,
Shall, stiff and stark and cold, appear like death;
And in this borrow'd likeness of shrunk death
Thou shalt continue two-and-forty hours,
And then awake as from a pleasant sleep.
Now, when the bridegroom in the morning comes
To rouse thee from thy bed, there art thou dead:
Then—as the manner of our country is—
In thy best robes uncover'd on the bier,
Thou shalt be borne to that same ancient vault
Where all the kindred of the Capulets lie.
In the mean time, against thou shalt awake,
Shall Romeo by my letters know our drift,
And hither shall he come; and he and I
Will watch thy waking, and that very night
Shall Romeo bear thee hence to Mantua.
And this shall free thee from this present shame;
If no unconstant toy, nor womanish fear,
Abate thy valour in the acting it.

JULIET. Give me, give me! O! tell me not of fear!

FRIAR LAURENCE. Hold; get you gone, be strong and prosperous
In this resolve. I'll send a friar with speed
To Mantua, with my letters to thy lord.

JULIET. Love, give me strength! and strength shall help afford.
Farewell, dear father!   *Exit*

SCENE TWO

Hall in Capulet's House.

Enter Capulet, Lady Capulet, Nurse, and Servingmen

CAPULET. So many guests invite as here are writ.   *Exit Servant*
Sirrah, go hire me twenty cunning cooks.

SECOND SERVANT. You shall have none ill, sir; for I'll try if they can lick
their fingers.

CAPULET. How canst thou try them so?

SECOND SERVANT. Marry, sir, 'tis an ill cook that cannot lick his own fingers: therefore he that cannot lick his fingers goes not with me.

CAPULET. Go, be gone.   *Exit Second Servant*

We shall be much unfurnish'd for this time.
What! is my daughter gone to Friar Laurence?

NURSE. Ay, forsooth.

CAPULET. Well, he may chance to do some good on her:
A peevish self-will'd harlotry it is.

NURSE. See where she comes from shrift with merry look.

Enter Juliet

CAPULET. How now, my headstrong! where have you been gadding?

JULIET. Where I have learn'd me to repent the sin
Of disobedient opposition
To you and your behests; and am enjoin'd
By holy Laurence to fall prostrate here,
And beg your pardon. Pardon, I beseech you!
Henceforward I am ever rul'd by you.

CAPULET. Send for the county; go tell him of this:
I'll have this knot knit up to-morrow morning.

JULIET. I met the youthful lord at Laurence' cell;
And gave him what becomed love I might,
Not stepping o'er the bounds of modesty.

CAPULET. Why, I'm glad on 't; this is well: stand up:
This is as 't should be. Let me see the county;
Ay, marry, go, I say, and fetch him hither.
Now, afore God! this reverend holy friar,
All our whole city is much bound to him.

JULIET. Nurse, will you go with me into my closet,
To help me sort such needful ornaments
As you think fit to furnish me to-morrow?

LADY CAPULET. No, not till Thursday; there is time enough.

CAPULET. Go, nurse, go with her. We'll to church tomorrow.

Exeunt Juliet and Nurse

LADY CAPULET. We shall be short in our provision:
'Tis now near night.

CAPULET.   Tush! I will stir about,
And all things shall be well, I warrant thee, wife:
Go thou to Juliet, help to deck up her;
I'll not to bed to-night; let me alone;
I'll play the housewife for this once. What, ho!
They are all forth: well, I will walk myself
To County Paris, to prepare him up

Against to-morrow. My heart is wondrous light,
Since this same wayward girl is so reclaim'd.   *Exeunt*

SCENE THREE

Juliet's Chamber.

Enter Juliet and Nurse

JULIET. Ay, those attires are best; but, gentle nurse,
  I pray thee, leave me to myself to-night;
  For I have need of many orisons
  To move the heavens to smile upon my state,
  Which, well thou know'st, is cross and full of sin.

Enter Lady Capulet

LADY CAPULET. What! are you busy, ho? need you my help?

JULIET. No, madam; we have cull'd such necessaries
  As are behoveful for our state to-morrow:
  So please you, let me now be left alone,
  And let the nurse this night sit up with you;
  For, I am sure, you have your hands full all
  In this so sudden business.

LADY CAPULET.   Good-night:
  Get thee to bed, and rest; for thou hast need.

Exeunt Lady Capulet and Nurse

JULIET. Farewell! God knows when we shall meet again.
  I have a faint cold fear thrills through my veins,
  That almost freezes up the heat of life:
  I'll call them back again to comfort me:
  Nurse! What should she do here?
  My dismal scene I needs must act alone.
  Come, vial.
  What if this mixture do not work at all?
  Shall I be married then to-morrow morning?
  No, no; this shall forbid it: lie thou there.   *Laying down a dagger*
  What if it be a poison, which the friar
  Subtly hath minister'd to have me dead,
  Lest in this marriage he should be dishonour'd
  Because he married me before to Romeo?
  I fear it is: and yet, methinks, it should not,
  For he hath still been tried a holy man.

I will not entertain so bad a thought.
How if, when I am laid into the tomb,
I wake before the time that Romeo
Come to redeem me? there's a fearful point!
Shall I not then be stifled in the vault,
To whose foul mouth no healthsome air breathes in,
And there die strangled ere my Romeo comes?
Or, if I live, is it not very like,
The horrible conceit of death and night,
Together with the terror of the place,
As in a vault, an ancient receptacle,
Where, for these many hundred years, the bones
Of all my buried ancestors are pack'd;
Where bloody Tybalt, yet but green in earth,
Lies festering in his shroud; where, as they say,
At some hours in the night spirits resort:
Alack, alack! is it not like that I,
So early waking, what with loathsome smells,
And shrieks like mandrakes' torn out of the earth,
That living mortals, hearing them, run mad:
O! if I wake, shall I not be distraught,
Environed with all these hideous fears,
And madly play with my forefathers' joints,
And pluck the mangled Tybalt from his shroud?
And, in this rage, with some great kinsman's bone,
As with a club, dash out my desperate brains?
O, look! methinks I see my cousin's ghost
Seeking out Romeo, that did spit his body
Upon a rapier's point. Stay, Tybalt, stay!
Romeo, I come! this do I drink to thee.

She falls upon her bed within the curtains

SCENE FOUR

Hall in Capulet's House.

Enter Lady Capulet and Nurse

LADY CAPULET. Hold, take these keys, and fetch more spices, nurse.
NURSE. They call for dates and quinces in the pastry.

Enter Capulet

CAPULET. Come, stir, stir, stir! the second cock hath crow'd,
   The curfew bell hath rung, 'tis three o'clock:
   Look to the bak'd meats, good Angelica:
   Spare not for cost.

NURSE.   Go, go, you cot-quean, go;
   Get you to bed; faith, you'll be sick to-morrow
   For this night's watching.

CAPULET. No, not a whit; what! I have watch'd ere now
   All night for lesser cause, and ne'er been sick.

LADY CAPULET. Ay, you have been a mouse-hunt in your time;
   But I will watch you from such watching now.

                              Exeunt Lady Capulet and Nurse

CAPULET. A jealous-hood, a jealous-hood!

           Enter three or four Servingmen, with spits,
                       logs, and baskets

                              Now, fellow,
   What's there?

FIRST SERVINGMAN. Things for the cook, sir; but I know not what.

CAPULET. Make haste, make haste.   *Exit first Servingman*
   Sirrah, fetch drier logs:
   Call Peter, he will show thee where they are.

SECOND SERVINGMAN. I have a head, sir, that will find out logs,
   And never trouble Peter for the matter.   *Exit*

CAPULET. Mass, and well said; a merry whoreson, ha!
   Thou shalt be logger-head. Good faith! 'tis day:
   The county will be here with music straight,
   For so he said he would. (*Music within*) I hear him near.
   Nurse! Wife! what, ho! What, nurse, I say!

                       Re-enter Nurse

   Go waken Juliet, go and trim her up;
   I'll go and chat with Paris. Hie, make haste,
   Make haste; the bridegroom he is come already:
   Make haste, I say.   *Exeunt*

SCENE FIVE

Juliet's Chamber.
Enter Nurse

NURSE. Mistress! what, mistress! Juliet! fast, I warrant her, she:
  Why, lamb! why, lady! fie, you slug-a-bed!
  Why, love, I say! madam! sweet-heart! why, bride!
  What! not a word? you take your pennyworths now:
  Sleep for a week; for the next night, I warrant,
  The County Paris hath set up his rest,
  That you shall rest but little. God forgive me,
  Marry, and amen, how sound is she asleep!
  I needs must wake her. Madam, madam, madam!
  Ay, let the county take you in your bed;
  He'll fright you up, i' faith. Will it not be?
  What, dress'd! and in your clothes! and down again!
  I must needs wake you. Lady! lady! lady!
  Alas! alas! Help! help! my lady's dead!
  O! well-a-day, that ever I was born.
  Some aqua-vitæ, ho! My lord! my lady!

Enter Lady Capulet

LADY CAPULET. What noise is here?
NURSE.   O lamentable day!
LADY CAPULET. What is the matter?
NURSE.   Look, look! O heavy day!
LADY CAPULET. O me, O me! my child, my only life,
  Revive, look up, or I will die with thee!
  Help, help! Call help.

Enter Capulet

CAPULET. For shame! bring Juliet forth; her lord is come.
NURSE. She's dead, deceas'd, she's dead; alack the day!
LADY CAPULET. Alack the day! she's dead! she's dead! she's dead!
CAPULET. Ha! let me see her. Out, alas! she's cold;
  Her blood is settled, and her joints are stiff;
  Life and these lips have long been separated:
  Death lies on her like an untimely frost
  Upon the sweetest flower of all the field.
NURSE. O lamentable day!
LADY CAPULET.   O woeful time!

CAPULET. Death, that hath ta'en her hence to make me wail,
    Ties up my tongue, and will not let me speak.
           Enter Friar Laurence, and Paris, with Musicians
FRIAR LAURENCE. Come, is the bride ready to go to church?
CAPULET. Ready to go, but never to return.
    O son! the night before thy wedding-day
    Hath Death lain with thy wife. There she lies,
    Flower as she was, deflowered by him.
    Death is my son-in-law, Death is my heir;
    My daughter he hath wedded: I will die,
    And leave him all; life, living, all is Death's!
PARIS. Have I thought long to see this morning's face,
    And doth it give me such a sight as this?
LADY CAPULET. Accurs'd, unhappy, wretched, hateful day!
    Most miserable hour that e'er time saw
    In lasting labour of his pilgrimage!
    But one, poor one, one poor and loving child,
    But one thing to rejoice and solace in,
    And cruel death hath catch'd it from my sight!
NURSE. O woe! O woeful, woeful, woeful day!
    Most lamentable day, most woeful day,
    That ever, ever, I did yet behold!
    O day! O day! O day! O hateful day!
    Never was seen so black a day as this:
    O woeful day, O woeful day!
PARIS. Beguil'd, divorced, wronged, spited, slain!
    Most detestable death, by thee beguil'd,
    By cruel cruel thee quite overthrown!
    O love! O life! not life, but love in death!
CAPULET. Despis'd, distressed, hated, martyr'd, kill'd!
    Uncomfortable time, why cam'st thou now
    To murder, murder our solemnity?
    O child! O child! my soul, and not my child!
    Dead art thou! dead! alack, my child is dead;
    And with my child my joys are buried!
FRIAR LAURENCE. Peace, ho! for shame! confusion's cure lives not
    In these confusions. Heaven and yourself
    Had part in this fair maid; now heaven hath all,
    And all the better is it for the maid:

Your part in her you could not keep from death,
But heaven keeps his part in eternal life.
The most you sought was her promotion,
For 'twas your heaven she should be advanc'd;
And weep ye now, seeing she is advanc'd
Above the clouds, as high as heaven itself?
O! in this love, you love your child so ill,
That you run mad, seeing that she is well:
She's not well married that lives married long;
But she's best married that dies married young.
Dry up your tears, and stick your rosemary
On this fair corse; and, as the custom is,
In all her best array bear her to church;
For though fond nature bids us all lament,
Yet nature's tears are reason's merriment.

CAPULET. All things that we ordained festival,
Turn from their office to black funeral;
Our instruments to melancholy bells,
Our wedding cheer to a sad burial feast,
Our solemn hymns to sullen dirges change,
Our bridal flowers serve for a buried corse,
And all things change them to the contrary.

FRIAR LAURENCE. Sir, go you in; and, madam, go with him;
And go, Sir Paris; every one prepare
To follow this fair corse unto her grave.
The heavens do lower upon you for some ill;
Move them no more by crossing their high will.

Exeunt Capulet, Lady Capulet, Paris, and Friar

FIRST MUSICIAN. Faith, we may put up our pipes, and be gone.

NURSE. Honest good fellows, ah! put up, put up, for, well you know, this is
a pitiful case. *Exit*

FIRST MUSICIAN. Ay, by my troth, the case may be amended.

Enter Peter

PETER. Musicians! O! musicians, "Heart's ease, Heart's ease": O! an ye will
have me live, play "Heart's ease."

FIRST MUSICIAN. Why "Heart's ease"?

PETER. O! musicians, because my heart itself plays "My heart is full of
woe"; O! play me some merry dump, to comfort me.

SECOND MUSICIAN. Not a dump we; 'tis no time to play now.

PETER. You will not then?

MUSICIANS. No.

PETER. I will then give it you soundly.

FIRST MUSICIAN. What will you give us?

PETER. No money, on my faith! but the gleek; I will give you the minstrel.

FIRST MUSICIAN. Then will I give you the serving-creature.

PETER. Then will I lay the serving-creature's dagger on your pate, I will
    carry no crotchets: I'll re you, I'll fa you. Do you note me?

FIRST MUSICIAN. An you re us, and fa us, you note us.

SECOND MUSICIAN. Pray you, put up your dagger, and put out your wit.

PETER. Then have at you with my wit! I will dry-beat you with an iron
    wit, and put up my iron dagger. Answer me like men:
        "When gripping grief the heart doth wound,
            And doleful dumps the mind oppress,
        Then music with her silver sound—"
    Why "silver sound"? why "music with her silver sound"?
    What say you, Simon Catling?

FIRST MUSICIAN. Marry, sir, because silver hath a sweet sound.

PETER. Pretty! What say you, Hugh Rebeck?

SECOND MUSICIAN. I say "silver sound," because musicians sound for
    silver.

PETER. Pretty too! What say you, James Soundpost?

THIRD MUSICIAN. Faith, I know not what to say.

PETER. O! I cry you mercy; you are the singer; I will say for you. It is,
    "music with her silver sound," because musicians have no gold for
    sounding:
        Then music with her silver sound
            With speedy help doth lend redress.   *Exit*

FIRST MUSICIAN. What a pestilent knave is this same!

SECOND MUSICIAN. Hang him, Jack! Come, we'll in here; tarry for the
    mourners, and stay dinner.   *Exeunt*

Act Five

SCENE ONE

Mantua. A Street.

Enter Romeo

ROMEO. If I may trust the flattering truth of sleep,
My dreams presage some joyful news at hand:
My bosom's lord sits lightly in his throne;
And all this day an unaccustom'd spirit
Lifts me above the ground with cheerful thoughts.
I dreamt my lady came and found me dead;—
Strange dream, that gives a dead man leave to think,—
And breath'd such life with kisses in my lips,
That I reviv'd, and was an emperor.
Ah me! how sweet is love itself possess'd,
When but love's shadows are so rich in joy!

Enter Balthasar, booted

News from Verona! How now, Balthasar?
Dost thou not bring me letters from the friar?
How doth my lady? Is my father well?
How fares my Juliet? That I ask again;
For nothing can be ill if she be well.

BALTHASAR. Then she is well, and nothing can be ill;
Her body sleeps in Capel's monument,
And her immortal part with angels lives.
I saw her laid low in her kindred's vault,
And presently took post to tell it you.
O! pardon me for bringing these ill news,
Since you did leave it for my office, sir.

ROMEO. Is it even so? then I defy you, stars!
　　Thou know'st my lodging: get me ink and paper,
　　And hire post-horses; I will hence to-night.
BALTHASAR. I do beseech you, sir, have patience:
　　Your looks are pale and wild, and do import
　　Some misadventure.
ROMEO.　　　　　　　Tush, thou art deceiv'd;
　　Leave me, and do the thing I bid thee do.
　　Hast thou no letters to me from the friar?
BALTHASAR. No, my good lord.
ROMEO.　　　　　　　　　　No matter; get thee gone,
　　And hire those horses: I'll be with thee straight.　　　　*Exit Balthasar*
　　Well, Juliet, I will lie with thee to-night.
　　Let's see for means: O mischief! thou art swift
　　To enter in the thoughts of desperate men.
　　I do remember an apothecary,
　　And hereabouts he dwells, which late I noted
　　In tatter'd weeds, with overwhelming brows,
　　Culling of simples; meagre were his looks,
　　Sharp misery had worn him to the bones:
　　And in his needy shop a tortoise hung,
　　An alligator stuff'd, and other skins
　　Of ill-shap'd fishes; and about his shelves
　　A beggarly account of empty boxes,
　　Green earthen pots, bladders, and musty seeds,
　　Remnants of packthread, and old cakes of roses,
　　Were thinly scatter'd, to make up a show.
　　Noting this penury, to myself I said
　　An if a man did need a poison now,
　　Whose sale is present death in Mantua,
　　Here lives a caitiff wretch would sell it him.
　　O! this same thought did but fore-run my need,
　　And this same needy man must sell it me.
　　As I remember, this should be the house:
　　Being holiday, the beggar's shop is shut.
　　What, ho! apothecary!
　　　　　　　　　Enter Apothecary
APOTHECARY.　　　　　Who calls so loud?
ROMEO. Come hither, man. I see that thou art poor;

Hold, there is forty ducats; let me have
A dram of poison, such soon-speeding gear
As will disperse itself through all the veins
That the life-weary taker may fall dead,
And that the trunk may be discharg'd of breath
As violently as hasty powder fir'd
Doth hurry from the fatal cannon's womb.

APOTHECARY. Such mortal drugs I have: but Mantua's law
Is death to any he that utters them.

ROMEO. Art thou so bare, and full of wretchedness,
And fear'st to die? famine is in thy cheeks,
Need and oppression starveth in thine eyes,
Contempt and beggary hang upon thy back;
The world is not thy friend nor the world's law:
The world affords no law to make thee rich;
Then be not poor, but break it, and take this.

APOTHECARY. My poverty, but not my will, consents.

ROMEO. I pay thy poverty, and not thy will.

APOTHECARY. Put this in any liquid thing you will,
And drink it off; and, if you had the strength
Of twenty men, it would dispatch you straight.

ROMEO. There is thy gold, worse poison to men's souls,
Doing more murders in this loathsome world
Than these poor compounds that thou mayst not sell:
I sell thee poison, thou hast sold me none.
Farewell; buy food, and get thyself in flesh.
Come, cordial and not poison, go with me
To Juliet's grave, for there must I use thee.   *Exeunt*

SCENE TWO

Verona. Friar Laurence's Cell.
Enter Friar John

FRIAR JOHN. Holy Franciscan friar; brother, ho!
Enter Friar Laurence

FRIAR LAURENCE. This same should be the voice of Friar John.
Welcome from Mantua: what says Romeo?
Or, if his mind be writ, give me his letter.

FRIAR JOHN. Going to find a bare-foot brother out,
  One of our order, to associate me,
  Here in this city visiting the sick,
  And finding him, the searchers of the town,
  Suspecting that we both were in a house,
  Where the infectious pestilence did reign,
  Seal'd up the doors, and would not let us forth;
  So that my speed to Mantua there was stay'd.
FRIAR LAURENCE. Who bare my letter then to Romeo?
FRIAR JOHN. I could not send it, here it is again,
  Nor get a messenger to bring it thee,
  So fearful were they of infection.
FRIAR LAURENCE. Unhappy fortune! by my brotherhood,
  The letter was not nice, but full of charge
  Of dear import; and the neglecting it
  May do much danger. Friar John, go hence;
  Get me an iron crow, and bring it straight
  Unto my cell.
FRIAR JOHN. Brother, I'll go and bring it thee.   *Exit*
FRIAR LAURENCE. Now must I to the monument alone;
  Within these three hours will fair Juliet wake:
  She will beshrew me much that Romeo
  Hath had no notice of these accidents;
  But I will write again to Mantua,
  And keep her at my cell till Romeo come:
  Poor living corse, clos'd in a dead man's tomb!   *Exit*

SCENE THREE

**Verona. A Churchyard; in it a Monument
belonging to the Capulets.**
Enter Paris, and his Page, bearing flowers and a torch
PARIS. Give me thy torch, boy: hence, and stand aloof;
  Yet put it out, for I would not be seen.
  Under yond yew-trees lay thee all along,
  Holding thine ear close to the hollow ground:
  So shall no foot upon the churchyard tread,
  Being loose, unfirm with digging up of graves,

But thou shalt hear it: whistle then to me,
As signal that thou hear'st something approach.
Give me those flowers. Do as I bid thee; go.

PAGE. (*Aside*) I am almost afraid to stand alone
Here in the churchyard; yet I will adventure. *Retires*

PARIS. Sweet flower, with flowers thy bridal bed I strew,—
O woe! thy canopy is dust and stones;—
Which with sweet water nightly I will dew,
Or, wanting that, with tears distill'd by moans:
The obsequies that I for thee will keep
Nightly shall be to strew thy grave and weep. *The Page whistles*
The boy gives warning something doth approach.
What cursed foot wanders this way to-night,
To cross my obsequies and true love's rite?
What! with a torch?—muffle me, night, awhile. *Retires*

Enter Romeo and Balthasar, with a torch, mattock, &c.

ROMEO. Give me that mattock, and the wrenching iron.
Hold, take this letter; early in the morning
See thou deliver it to my lord and father.
Give me the light: upon thy life I charge thee,
Whate'er thou hear'st or seest, stand all aloof,
And do not interrupt me in my course.
Why I descend into this bed of death,
Is partly to behold my lady's face;
But chiefly to take thence from her dead finger
A precious ring, a ring that I must use
In dear employment: therefore hence, be gone:
But, if thou, jealous, dost return to pry
In what I further shall intend to do,
By heaven, I will tear thee joint by joint,
And strew this hungry churchyard with thy limbs.
The time and my intents are savage-wild,
More fierce and more inexorable far
Than empty tigers or the roaring sea.

BALTHASAR. I will be gone, sir, and not trouble you.

ROMEO. So shalt thou show me friendship. Take thou that:
Live, and be prosperous; and farewell, good fellow.

BALTHASAR. (*Aside*) For all this same, I'll hide me here about:
His looks I fear, and his intents I doubt. *Retires*

ROMEO. Thou detestable maw, thou womb of death,
    Gorg'd with the dearest morsel of the earth,
    Thus I enforce thy rotten jaws to open,   *Opens the tomb*
    And, in despite, I'll cram thee with more food!
PARIS. This is that banish'd haughty Montague,
    That murder'd my love's cousin, with which grief
    It is supposed the fair creature died;
    And here is come to do some villanous shame
    To the dead bodies: I will apprehend him.—   *Comes forward*
    Stop thy unhallow'd toil, vile Montague,
    Can vengeance be pursu'd further than death?
    Condemned villain, I do apprehend thee:
    Obey, and go with me; for thou must die.
ROMEO. I must, indeed; and therefore came I hither.
    Good gentle youth, tempt not a desperate man;
    Fly hence and leave me: think upon these gone;
    Let them affright thee. I beseech thee, youth,
    Put not another sin upon my head
    By urging me to fury: O! be gone:
    By heaven, I love thee better than myself,
    For I come hither arm'd against myself:
    Stay not, be gone; live, and hereafter say
    A madman's mercy bade thee run away.
PARIS. I do defy thy conjurations,
    And apprehend thee for a felon here.
ROMEO. Wilt thou provoke me? then have at thee, boy!   *They fight*
PAGE. O Lord! they fight: I will go call the watch.   *Exit*
PARIS. (*Falls*) O, I am slain!—If thou be merciful,
    Open the tomb, lay me with Juliet.   *Dies*
ROMEO. In faith, I will. Let me peruse this face:
    Mercutio's kinsman, noble County Paris!
    What said my man when my betossed soul
    Did not attend him as we rode? I think
    He told me Paris should have married Juliet:
    Said he not so? or did I dream it so?
    Or am I mad, hearing him talk of Juliet,
    To think it was so? O! give me thy hand,
    One writ with me in sour misfortune's book:
    I'll bury thee in a triumphant grave;

A grave? O, no! a lanthorn, slaughter'd youth,
For here lies Juliet, and her beauty makes
This vault a feasting presence full of light.
Death, lie thou there, by a dead man interr'd.   *Laying Paris in the tomb*
How oft when men are at the point of death
Have they been merry! which their keepers call
A lightning before death: O! how may I
Call this a lightning? O my love! my wife!
Death, that hath suck'd the honey of thy breath,
Hath had no power yet upon thy beauty:
Thou art not conquer'd; beauty's ensign yet
Is crimson in thy lips and in thy cheeks,
And death's pale flag is not advanced there.
Tybalt, liest thou there in thy bloody sheet?
O! what more favour can I do to thee,
Than with that hand that cut thy youth in twain
To sunder his that was thine enemy?
Forgive me, cousin! Ah! dear Juliet,
Why art thou yet so fair? Shall I believe
That unsubstantial Death is amorous,
And that the lean abhorred monster keeps
Thee here in dark to be his paramour?
For fear of that I still will stay with thee,
And never from this palace of dim night
Depart again: here, here will I remain
With worms that are thy chambermaids; O! here
Will I set up my everlasting rest,
And shake the yoke of inauspicious stars
From this world-wearied flesh. Eyes, look your last!
Arms, take your last embrace! and, lips, O you
The doors of breath, seal with a righteous kiss
A dateless bargain to engrossing death!
Come, bitter conduct, come, unsavory guide!
Thou desperate pilot, now at once run on
The dashing rocks thy sea-sick weary bark!
Here's to my love! (*Drinks*) O true apothecary!
Thy drugs are quick. Thus with a kiss I die.   *Dies*

> *Enter, at the other end of the Churchyard, Friar*
> *Laurence, with a lanthorn, crow, and spade*

FRIAR LAURENCE. Saint Francis be my speed! how oft tonight
  Have my old feet stumbled at graves! Who's there?
BALTHASAR. Here's one, a friend, and one that knows you well.
FRIAR LAURENCE. Bliss be upon you! Tell me, good my friend,
  What torch is yond, that vainly lends his light
  To grubs and eyeless skulls? as I discern,
  It burneth in the Capel's monument.
BALTHASAR. It doth so, holy sir; and there's my master,
  One that you love.
FRIAR LAURENCE. Who is it?
BALTHASAR.   Romeo.
FRIAR LAURENCE. How long hath he been there?
BALTHASAR.   Full half an hour.
FRIAR LAURENCE. Go with me to the vault.
BALTHASAR.   I dare not, sir.
  My master knows not but I am gone hence;
  And fearfully did menace me with death
  If I did stay to look on his intents.
FRIAR LAURENCE. Stay then, I'll go alone. Fear comes upon me;
  O! much I fear some ill unlucky thing.
BALTHASAR. As I did sleep under this yew-tree here,
  I dreamt my master and another fought,
  And that my master slew him.
FRIAR LAURENCE. (*Advances*) Romeo!
  Alack, alack! what blood is this which stains
  The stony entrance of this sepulchre?
  What mean these masterless and gory swords
  To lie discolour'd by this place of peace?   *Enters the tomb*
  Romeo! O pale! Who else? what! Paris too?
  And steep'd in blood? Ah! what an unkind hour
  Is guilty of this lamentable chance.
  The lady stirs.   *Juliet wakes*
JULIET. O, comfortable friar! where is my lord?
  I do remember well where I should be,
  And there I am. Where is my Romeo?   *Noise within*
FRIAR LAURENCE. I hear some noise. Lady, come from that nest
  Of death, contagion, and unnatural sleep:
  A greater power than we can contradict
  Hath thwarted our intents: come, come away.

Thy husband in thy bosom there lies dead:
And Paris too: come, I'll dispose of thee
Among a sisterhood of holy nuns.
Stay not to question, for the watch is coming;
Come, go, good Juliet.—(*Noise again*) I dare no longer stay.

JULIET. Go, get thee hence, for I will not away.   *Exit Friar Laurence*
What's here? a cup, clos'd in my true love's hand?
Poison, I see, hath been his timeless end.
O churl! drunk all, and left no friendly drop
To help me after! I will kiss thy lips;
Haply, some poison yet doth hang on them,
To make me die with a restorative.   *Kisses him*
Thy lips are warm!

FIRST WATCH. (*Within*) Lead, boy: which way?

JULIET. Yea, noise? then I'll be brief. O happy dagger!
     Snatching Romeo's dagger
This is thy sheath; (*Stabs herself.*) there rest, and let me die.
     Falls on Romeo's body and dies

     Enter Watch, with the Page of Paris

PAGE. This is the place; there where the torch doth burn.

FIRST WATCH. The ground is bloody; search about the churchyard.
Go, some of you; who'er you find, attach.   *Exeunt some of the Watch*
Pitiful sight! here lies the county slain,
And Juliet bleeding, warm, and newly dead,
Who here hath lain these two days buried.
Go, tell the prince, run to the Capulets,
Raise up the Montagues, some others search: *Exeunt others of the Watch*
We see the ground whereon these woes do lie;
But the true ground of all these piteous woes
We cannot without circumstance descry.

     Re-enter some of the Watch, with Balthasar

SECOND WATCH. Here's Romeo's man; we found him in the churchyard.

FIRST WATCH. Hold him in safety, till the prince come hither.

     Re-enter other of the Watch, with Friar Laurence

THIRD WATCH. Here is a friar, that trembles, sighs, and weeps;
We took this mattock and this spade from him,
As he was coming from this churchyard side.

FIRST WATCH. A great suspicion: stay the friar too.

Enter the Prince and Attendants

PRINCE. What misadventure is so early up,
  That calls our person from our morning's rest?

Enter Capulet, Lady Capulet, and Others

CAPULET. What should it be, that they so shriek abroad?

LADY CAPULET. The people in the street cry Romeo,
  Some Juliet, and some Paris; and all run
  With open outcry toward our monument.

PRINCE. What fear is this which startles in our ears?

FIRST WATCH. Sovereign, here lies the County Paris slain;
  And Romeo dead; and Juliet, dead before,
  Warm and new kill'd.

PRINCE. Search, seek, and know how this foul murder comes.

FIRST WATCH. Here is a friar, and slaughter'd Romeo's man;
  With instruments upon them, fit to open
  These dead men's tombs.

CAPULET. O, heaven!—O wife! look how our daughter bleeds!
  This dagger hath mista'en!—for, lo, his house
  Is empty on the back of Montague—
  And is mis-sheathed in my daughter's bosom.

LADY CAPULET. O me! this sight of death is as a bell,
  That warns my old age to a sepulchre.

Enter Montague and Others

PRINCE. Come, Montague: for thou art early up,
  To see thy son and heir more early down.

MONTAGUE. Alas! my liege, my wife is dead to-night;
  Grief of my son's exile hath stopp'd her breath.
  What further woe conspires against mine age?

PRINCE. Look, and thou shalt see.

MONTAGUE. O thou untaught! what manners is in this,
  To press before thy father to a grave?

PRINCE. Seal up the mouth of outrage for a while,
  Till we can clear these ambiguities,
  And know their spring, their head, their true descent;
  And then will I be general of your woes,
  And lead you even to death: meantime forbear,
  And let mischance be slave to patience.
  Bring forth the parties of suspicion.

FRIAR LAURENCE. I am the greatest, able to do least,
    Yet most suspected, as the time and place
    Doth make against me, of this direful murder;
    And here I stand, both to impeach and purge
    Myself condemned and myself excus'd.
PRINCE. Then say at once what thou dost know in this.
FRIAR LAURENCE. I will be brief, for my short date of breath
    Is not so long as is a tedious tale.
    Romeo, there dead, was husband to that Juliet;
    And she, there dead, that Romeo's faithful wife:
    I married them; and their stolen marriage-day
    Was Tybalt's doomsday, whose untimely death
    Banish'd the new-made bridegroom from this city;
    For whom, and not for Tybalt, Juliet pin'd.
    You, to remove that siege of grief from her,
    Betroth'd, and would have married her perforce,
    To County Paris: then comes she to me,
    And, with wild looks bid me devise some mean
    To rid her from this second marriage,
    Or in my cell there would she kill herself.
    Then gave I her,—so tutor'd by my art,—
    A sleeping potion; which so took effect
    As I intended, for it wrought on her
    The form of death: meantime I writ to Romeo
    That he should hither come as this dire night,
    To help to take her from her borrow'd grave,
    Being the time the potion's force should cease.
    But he which bore my letter, Friar John,
    Was stay'd by accident, and yesternight
    Return'd my letter back. Then, all alone,
    At the prefixed hour of her waking,
    Came I to take her from her kindred's vault,
    Meaning to keep her closely at my cell,
    Till I conveniently could send to Romeo:
    But, when I came,—some minute ere the time
    Of her awakening,—here untimely lay
    The noble Paris and true Romeo dead.
    She wakes; and I entreated her come forth,
    And bear this work of heaven with patience;

But then a noise did scare me from the tomb,
And she, too desperate, would not go with me,
But, as it seems, did violence on herself.
All this I know; and to the marriage
Her nurse is privy: and, if aught in this
Miscarried by my fault, let my old life
Be sacrific'd, some hour before his time,
Unto the rigour of severest law.

PRINCE. We still have known thee for a holy man.
Where's Romeo's man? what can he say in this?

BALTHASAR. I brought my master news of Juliet's death;
And then in post he came from Mantua
To this same place, to this same monument.
This letter he early bid me give his father,
And threaten'd me with death, going in the vault,
If I departed not and left him there.

PRINCE. Give me the letter; I will look on it.
Where is the county's page that rais'd the watch?
Sirrah, what made your master in this place?

PAGE. He came with flowers to strew his lady's grave,
And bid me stand aloof, and so I did;
Anon, comes one with light to ope the tomb;
And by and by my master drew on him;
And then I ran away to call the watch.

PRINCE. This letter doth make good the friar's words,
Their course of love, the tidings of her death;
And here he writes that he did buy a poison
Of a poor 'pothecary, and therewithal
Came to this vault to die, and lie with Juliet.
Where be these enemies?—Capulet! Montague!
See what a scourge is laid upon your hate,
That heaven finds means to kill your joys with love;
And I, for winking at your discords too,
Have lost a brace of kinsmen: all are punish'd.

CAPULET. O brother Montague! give me thy hand:
This is my daughter's jointure, for no more
Can I demand.

MONTAGUE. But I can give thee more;
For I will raise her statue in pure gold;

That while Verona by that name is known,
There shall no figure at such rate be set
As that of true and faithful Juliet.
CAPULET. As rich shall Romeo by his lady lie;
   Poor sacrifices of our enmity!
PRINCE. A glooming peace this morning with it brings;
   The sun, for sorrow, will not show his head:
   Go hence, to have more talk of these sad things;
   Some shall be pardon'd, and some punished:
   For never was a story of more woe
   Than this of Juliet and her Romeo. *Exeunt*

NOTES

Prologue, omitted in Folios.

I. i. 18. *"cruel"*; so Quartos 4, 5; Quartos 2, 3, Folios read *"ciuil,"* and *"civil."*

I. i. 89. *"father"*; so Quartos 2, 4; Quarto 5, *"further"*; Quarto 3, Folios 1, 2, 3, *"Fathers"*; Folio 4, *"Father's."*

I. i. 108. *"drave me to walk abroad"*; Pope (from Quarto 1), *"drew me from company"*; Theobald, *"drew me to walk abroad."*

I. i. 115. *"Which then most sought where most might not be found"*; Pope (from Quarto 1), *"That most are busied, when they're most alone"*; Keightley, *"Which there ...,"* &c. Herr conjectured *"Which then most sought where many ..."*; Allen conjectured *"which then most sought where more ..."*

I. i. 140. *"sun"*; Theobald's emendation of Quartos and Folios, *"same."*

I. i. 161. *"see pathways to his will"*; Staunton conjectured *"set pathways to our will"*; Hanmer, *"... ill."*

I. i. 176. *"Why such is"*; Seymour conjectured *"Why such is, merely"*; Collier MS., *"Why such, Benvolio, is"*; Mommsen conjectured *"Why, such, Benvolio, such is"*; Keightley, *"Why, gentle cousin, such is"*; Orger conjectured *"Why, such a love is."*

I. i. 181. *"raised"*; Pope's correction (from Quarto 1); Quartos, Folios, *"made."*

I. i. 195. *"Bid a sick man in sadness make"*; so (Quarto 1) Quartos 4, 5; Quartos 2, 3, Folio 1, read *"A sicke man in sadnesse makes"*; Folios 2, 3, 4, *"A sicke man in good sadnesse makes."*

I. i. 204. *"From love's weak childish bow she lives unharm'd"*; Grant White conjectured *" 'Gainst ... encharm'd"*; Quartos, Folios, *"vncharmd"*; Collier MS., *"encharm'd."*

I. i. 209. *"with beauty dies her store"*; Theobald reads *"with her dies Beauty's Store"*; Keightley, *"with her dies beauty store."*

I. ii. 15. *"She is the hopeful lady of my earth"*; Johnson conjectured *"She is the hope and stall of my full years."*

I. ii. 25. *"made dark heaven light"*; Theobald reads *"make dark heaven's light"*; Warburton, *"make dark even light"*; Jackson conjectured *"mask dark heaven's light"*; Daniel conjectured *"mock dark heaven's light."*

I. ii. 26. *"young men"*; Johnson conjectured *"yeomen."*

I. ii. 32. *"Which on more view,"* &c.; so Quartos 4, 5; Quartos 2, 3, Folios, *"one"* for *"on";* (Quarto 1) *"Such, amongst view of many myne being one";* perhaps we should read with Mason, *"Whilst on more view of many, mine being one";* many readings have been proposed.

I. iii. 37. *"Shake, quoth the dove-house,"* referring to the effects of the earthquake; Daniel conjectured *"goeth"* for *"quoth."*

I. iii. 70, 71. *"honour";* Pope's emendation (from Quarto 1); Quartos, Folios, *"houre"* and *"hour."*

I. iv. 39. *"The game was ne'er so fair, and I am done";* "an allusion to an old proverbial saying which advises to give over when the game is at the fairest" (Ritson).

I. iv. 41. *Cp.* Chaucer's *Manciple's Prologue:*——

> "Ther gan our hoste for to jape and pleye,
> And seyde, sirs, what!
> Dun is in the myre!"

A proverbial expression originally used in an old rural sport, and meaning, "we are all at a standstill!" or, "let us make an effort to move on" (*vide* Prof. Skeat's *Notes to Canterbury Tales,* Vol. v. p. 435–6).

I. iv. 42. *"Of this sir-reverence love";* Singer's emendation (from Quarto 1); Quartos read *"Or saue you reuerence loue";* Folios 1, 2, *3,* "Or saue flour reuerence loue."

I. iv. 43. Capell's emendation; (Quarto 1) reads *"We burne our lights by night, like Lampes by day";* Quartos, *"We waste our lights in vaine, lights lights by day";* Folios, *"We wast our lights in vaine, lights, lights, by day."*

I. iv. 71. *"Maid";* Pope's reading (from Quarto 1); Quartos, Folio 1, *"man";* Folios 2, 3, 4, *"woman";* Ulrici (from Collier MS.), *"milkmaid."*

I. iv. 82. *"Courtier's";* Pope (from Quarto 1) reads *"lawyer's";* Theobald conjectured *"taylor's."*

I. iv. 90. *"Of healths";* Thirlby conjectured *"Of delves";* Keightley conjectured *"Trenches";* Clark MS., *"Of hilts."*

I. iv. 96. *"Untangled"; "which once u.,"* the untangling of which.

I. iv. 104. *"Face";* Pope's reading (from Quarto 1); Quartos, Folios, *"side";* Collier MS., *"tide."*

I. v. 16. *"Will have a bout";* (Quarto 1); *"will haue about";* Quartos, Folios, *"will walke about";* Pope, *"we'll haue a bout";* Daniel, *"will walke a bout."*

I. v. 46. *"It seems she";* so (Quarto 1); Quartos, Folio 1; Folios 2, 3, 4, read *"Her beauty";* Bulloch conjectured *"In streams she";* &c.

II. i. 26. *"pronounce";* Quartos 2, 3, *"prouaunt";* Folio 1, *"Prouant";* Folios 2, 3, 4, *"Couply";* Rowe, *"couple."*

II. i. 29. *"trim,"* Steevens (from Quarto 1); Quartos, Folios, *"true."*

II. i. 29. *"Young Adam Cupid, he that shot so trim";* all the early editions read *"Abraham Cupid";* Theobald conjectured *"auborn";* Upton, *"Adam,"* referring to Adam Bell, the famous archer. It must be borne in mind, however, that *"Abram," "Abraham,"* was a regular corrupt form of *auburn,* formerly often written *abern, abron.*

II. ii. 43–44. *"nor any other part Belonging to a man. O, be some other name!"* Malone's emendation; Pope (from Quarto 1) reads *"nor any other part";* Quartos, Folios, *"O be some other name Belonging to a man."*

II. ii. 46. *"name,"* so Pope (from Quarto 1); Quartos, Folios, *"word."*

II. ii. 65. *"fair maid, if either thee dislike"*; so Quartos, Folios; Pope (from Quarto 1) reads *"fair saint ... displease"*; Theobald, *"fair saint ... dislike"*; Grant White, *"fair maid ... displease"*; Anon. conjectured *"fair maid ... mislike."*

II. ii. 111. *"blessed moon I swear"*; so (Quarto 1) Quartos; Folios read *"moon I vow."*

II. ii. 159. *"suit"*; so Quarto 5; Quarto 4, *"sute"*; Quartos 2, 3, Folios, *"strife."*

II. ii. 200. *"father's cell"*; Capell's reading (from Quarto 1); Quartos, Folios 3, 4, "*Friers close cell"*; Folios 1, 2, *"Fries close cell."*

II. iii. 1–4. Omitted in Folios 2, 3, 4.

II. iii. 4. *"day's path and Titan's fiery wheels"*; Malone's reading (from Quarto 1); Quartos, Folio 1, *"day's path, and Titans burning wheels"*; Pope, *"day's pathway, made by Titan's wheels."*

II. iii. 23. *"small,"* so Pope (from Quarto 1); Quartos, Folios, *"weake."*

II. iv. 124–125 *"I am none of his skains-mates"*; *"skains-mates"* occurs nowhere else, its origin is uncertain; it is perhaps connected with *skain, skein,* "as if associated in winding yarns" (or *skain's* = gen. of *skain, skean* = dagger; "as if a brother in arms").

II. vi. 34. *"sum up sum of half my"*; so Quartos 2, 3; Quartos 4, 5, *"summe up some of halfe my"*; Folios, *"sum up some of halfe my,"* &c.

III. i. 102. *"kinsman,"* Capell's reading (from Quarto 1); Quarto 5, other texts, *"cousin."*

III. i. 158. *"agile"*; (Quarto 1) Quartos 4, 5, *"agill"*; Quartos 2, 3, Folio 1, *"aged"*; Folios 2, 3, 4, *"able."*

III. i. 181. *"hate's"*; Knight's emendation; Quartos, Folios, read *"hearts"*; Hanmer, *"heats'"*; Johnson, *"hearts'."*

III. ii. 6. *"That runaways' eyes may wink"*; an epitome of the various interpretations of these words filling no less than twenty-eight pages of Furness's variorum edition; the Quartos and Folios do not mark the possessive, and scholars are divided on the subject of the singular or plural possessive. The Cambridge editors evidently make *"runaways"* = runagates, nightprowlers. The present editor cannot bring himself to believe that Shakespeare intended this reading, and would fain substitute *"Runaway's"* in the sense of "Day's"; "Runaway" may have belonged to the playful phraseology of Elizabethan girls, and savours of the expressive language of children's rhymes.

III. ii. 68. *"dear-loved"*; Pope's reading (from Quarto 1); Quartos, Folios, read *"dearest."*

III. ii. 78. *"Dove-feather'd raven"*; Theobald's emendation of Quartos 2, 3, Folio 1, *"Rauenous douefeathered Rauen"*; Quartos 4, 5, Folios 2, 3, 4, *"Rauenous doue, feathred Rauen."*

III. ii. 81. *"damned saint"*; so Quartos 4, 5, Folios 2, 3, 4; Quartos 2, 3, *"dimme saint"*; Folio 1, *"dimne saint."*

III. iii. 52. *"Thou fond mad man, hear me but speak a word"*; Malone's emendation (from Quarto 1); Quartos 2, 3, *"Then fond mad man, heare me a little speake"*;

Quartos 4, 5, *"Thou fond mad man, heare me a little speake"*; Folio 1, *"Then fond mad man, heare me speake"*; Folios 2, 3, 4, *"Fond mad man, heare me speake."*

III. v. 31. According to Warburton there is a popular saying to this effect, due to the fact that the toad has very fine eyes and the lark very ugly ones.

III. v. 55. *"below"*; Pope's reading (from Quarto 1); Quartos, Folios, *"so lowe."*

III. v. 155. Omitted in Folios.

III. v. 170. *"lent"*; Pope (from Quarto 1) reads *"sent"*; Cowden Clarke conjectured *"left."*

III. v. 185–188. So Quarto 2 and the other Quartos; Quarto 1 reads:—

    "Gods blessed mother wife it mads me,
      Day, night, early, late, at home, abroad,
      Alone, in company, waking or sleeping,
      Still my care hath been to see her matcht."

Many attempts have been made to smooth the lines, but perhaps they express Capulet's excitement.

III. v. 190. *"train'd"*; Capell's reading (from Quarto 1); Quartos 3, 4, 5, Folios *"allied"*; Quarto 2, *"liand"*; &c.

IV. i. 3. *"nothing slow to slack his haste"*; Collier conjectured *"something slow,"* &c.; Quarto 1, *"nothing slack to slow his haste"*; Johnson conjectured *"nothing slow to back his haste."*

IV. i. 17. Omitted in Quartos, Folios.

IV. i. 46. *"cure,"* so (Quarto 1) Quarto 5; Quartos 2, 3, 4, Folios, *"care."*

IV. i. 116–117. *"and he and I Will watch thy waking"*; the reading of Quartos 3, 4, 5; omitted in Folios.

IV. v. 107. *"O play me some merry dump, to comfort me"*; the reading of Quartos; omitted in Folios.

IV. v. 121–123. These lines are from Richard Edwards's *Paradise of Dainty Devises,* 1576.

V. i. 1. *"flattering truth"*; so Quartos, Folios; Malone following (Quarto 1) reads *"flattering eye"*; Collier MS., *"flattering death"*; Grant White, *"flattering sooth"*; &c.

V. i. 24. *"I defy you"*; Pope's reading; (Quarto 1), *"I defie my"*; Quartos 2, 3, 4, Folio 1, *"I denie you"*; Folios 2, 3, 4, Quarto 5, *"I deny you."*

V. i. 27. *"I do beseech you, sir, have patience"*; Pope (from Quarto 1) reads *"Pardon me sir, I dare not leave you thus"*; Steevens (1793) reads *"Pardon me, sir, I will not leave you thus."*

V. iii. 122. *"Stumbled at graves,"* &c:—

    "For many men that stumble at the threshold
    Are well foretold that danger lurks within";
                     3 Henry VI, IV. vii. 11, 12

V. iii. 175. *"rust"*; so Quartos, Folios; Hazlitt (from Quarto 1) reads *"rest."*

V. iii. 210. *"it,"* i.e., the dagger; so Quarto 2, the rest read *"is."*

—————— *"mis-sheathed"*; the reading of Folio 4; Folios 1, 2, 3, Quarto 5, *"misheathed"*; Quarto 3, 4, *"missheath'd"*; Jackson conjectured *"mi-sheath'd."*

V. iii. 215. After this line (Quarto 1) reads *"and young Benvolio is deceased too."*

GLOSSARY

abuse, ill-usage, offence. iii. 1; ill use, do violence to. iv. 1

accord, assent, consent. i. 2

Adam Cupid, Cupid the Archer (from Adam Bell, a famous archer). ii. 1

advance, raise, lift up. ii. 3; &c.

adventure, venture. ii. 2; v. 3

affray, frighten away. iii. 5

ally, kinsman, relative. iii. 1

ambuscado, ambush. i. 4

amerce, punish. iii. 1

anatomy, used depreciatively of the bodily frame. iii. 3

antic, antick, fantastic, grotesque. i. 5; ii. 4.

antres, caverns. Oth. 1. 3

aqua-vitae, ardent spirits. iv. 5

baked meats, meat pies. iv. 4

bandy, contend, fight. iii. 1; impel (as a ball). ii. 5

banquet, course of sweetmeats, fruit, and wine; dessert. i. 5

bate, in hawking, to beat the wings impatiently and flutter on the perch. iii. 2

bawd, hare. ii. 4

bear a brain, have remembrance. i. 3

becomed, becoming, befitting. iv. 2

bite the thumb, an insulting gesture. i. 1

blazon, describe fitly, publish the praises of. ii. 6

button, butcher of a silk, expert fencer. ii. 4

butt-shaft, unbarbed arrow used in shooting at the butts. ii. 4

cankered, (1) worm-eaten, (2) malignant. i. 1

carriage, power of or capacity for carrying. i. 4

carry, endure, put up with. iv. 5

case, mask, covering. i. 4

cause, term in duelling. ii. 4

centre, soul, as centre of the body. ii. 1

chance, unfortunate event. v. 3

chapless, lacking the lower jaw. iv. 1

charge, importance. v. 2

cheveril, kid-leather. ii. 4

chop-logic, contentious, sophistical arguer. iii. 5

civil, of or belonging to citizens. prol. 4

close, join. ii. 6; shut up, enclosed. iii. 2; v. 3

clout, piece of cloth, rag. ii. 4

clubs, a call to summon assistance. i. 1

coals, carry, submit to insult. i. 1

cock-a-hoop, set, give the rein to disorder. i. 5

cockatrice, basilisk, supposed to kill by its look. iii. 2

comfortable, affording comfort, consolation, help. v. 3

compliment, observance of ceremony, formal civility. ii. 2; &c.

concealed, secretly married. iii. 3

confidence, ? misuse for "conference." ii. 4

convoy, means of conveyance. ii. 4

cot-quean, man that busies himself with matters belonging to the wife's province. iv. 4

countervail, equal, counter-balance. ii. 6

court-cupboard, movable sideboard or cabinet. i. 5

coz, cousin. i. 5

crow, crowbar. v. 2

crow-keeper, one employed to keep crows away, scare-crow. i. 4

crush, discuss, drink. i. 2

curious, observant. i. 4

Cynthia, the moon-goddess. iii. 5

dainty, make, be chary or loth. i. 5

date, duration, term of existence. i. 4

dateless, endless. v. 3

dear, rare, ? loving. iii, 3; important. v. 2

defence, arms, armour. iii. 3

depend, impend, be imminent. iii. 1

dislike, displeased. ii. 2

dismal, disastrous, calamitous. iv. 3

distance, definite interval of space to be kept between fencers. ii. 4

distemperature, disturbance of mind. ii. 3

division, execution of a rapid passage of melody. iii. 5

drawer, tapster. iii. 1

dry-beat, to beat soundly. iii. 1; iv. 5

dump, tune. iv. 5

elf-locks, tangled mass of hair supposed to be due to the agency of elves. i. 4

endart, shoot as a dart. i. 3

engross, gain exclusive possession of, monopolize. v. 3

entreat, beguile, pass the time. iv. 1

exchange, thing offered or given in exchange. ii. 6

exhale, draw forth, esp. of the sun drawing up vapours and thereby producing meteors. iii. 5

fair, a phrase for a beautiful woman. ii. prol.

fantastico, absurd, irrational person. ii. 4

fashion-monger, one who studies and follows the fashion. ii. 4

fault, lack, want. ii. 4

fee-simple, estate belonging to the owner and his heirs for ever, absolute possession. iii. 1

fellow, mode of address to a servant. i. 2

fettle, make ready, prepare. iii. 5

fine, exquisitely fashioned, beautiful. ii. 1

fit, be fitting. i. 5

flecked, dappled. ii. 3

fleer, sneer, gibe. i. 5

flirt-gill, woman of light or loose behaviour. ii. 4

fool, used as a term of endearment or pity. i. 3; dupe, sport. iii. 1

gear, matter, affair, business. ii. 4; stuff. v. 1

ghostly, spiritual. iii. 3

give, attribute, assign. iv. 5

gleek, gibe, jest. iv. 5

gossip, applied to a woman's female friends invited to be present at a birth. iii. 5; friend. ii. 1

government, control, management. iv. 1

grace, virtue, efficacy. ii. 3

grandsire, ancient. i. 4

green, pale, sickly. ii. 2; fresh, late. iv. 3

grievance, trouble, distress, suffering. i. 1

ground, motive, reason. v. 3

halidom, by my, an asseveration. i. 3

hall, a, a cry to make room, e.g., for a dance. i. 5

hap, dear, good fortune. ii. 2

harlot, lewd person. ii. 4

harlotry, silly wench. iv. 2

have at, I will attack, begin. iv. 5

hay, home-thrust. ii. 4

heart's ease, name of a popular Elizabethan tune. iv. 5

high lone, quite alone. i. 3

hilding, jade, baggage. iii. 5

hoar, mouldy, become mouldy. ii. 4

hold, have, keep, be. ii. 2

hood-wink, blindfold. i. 4

humorous, moist, damp. ii. 1

humour, temper, quality. iv. 1

hunts-up, early morning sun. iii. 5
idle, move lazily or uselessly. ii. 6
imagined, having its seat in the mind. ii. 6
import, imply, indicate, express. v. 1
indite, misused for "invite." ii. 4
interest, concern, part. iii. 1
issue, decision, matter ripe for decision. iv. 1
Jack, low-bred fellow. ii. 4
jaunce, jauncing, trotting or trudging up and down. ii. 5
jealous-hood, ? jealous spy. iv. 4
joint-stool, kind of folding-chair. i. 5
keeper, sick nurse. v. 3
kindly, exactly. ii. 4
knit, bind, unite. iv. 2
lace, streak or stripe with colour. iii. 5
Lammas-eve, July 31. i. 3
Lammas-tide, Aug. 1. i. 3
lanthorn, window-turret. v. 3
large, licentious, gross. ii. 4
leave, used as a phrase of dismissal. i. 3
lenten, containing no meat. ii. 4
level, range of a missile, weapon. iii. 3
light, swift. ii. 2; full of levity. ii. 2
lure, recall a hawk to the lure. ii. 2
mammet, doll. iii. 5
manage, handle, wield. i. 1; contrive, contrivance. iii. 1
mandrake, poisonous plant, supposed to utter a shriek when pulled out of the
    ground. iv. 3
marchpane, marzipan. i. 5
margent, margin, commentary. i. 3
mark, God bless the, an expression of apology for the mention of something
    disagreeable, or of scorn. iii. 2
marry, unite, join closely. i. 3; orig. the name of the Blessed Virgin used as an
    exclamation or asseveration. ii 5; &c.
match, place in competition with. ii. chor. 4
meddle, have dealings, concern oneself. i. 2
medlar, fruit like a small brown-skinned apple. ii. 1
merchant, fellow. ii. 4
mew, coop up, shut up. iii. 4
mickle, great. ii. 3
mind, attend to. iv. 1
minim, musical note. ii. 4
minister, apply, administer, render aid. iv. 3
mistake, go astray. v. 3

mis-tempered, tempered for an evil purpose. i. 1
monument, place of burial, sepulchre. iii. 5
mood, anger, displeasure. iii. 1
motion, power of movement. iii. 2
mouse-hunt, woman-hunter. iv. 4
move, make angry. i. 1
mutiny, discord. i. 5
native, natural. iv. 1
naught, wicked, naughty. iii. 2; &c.
needly, of necessity. iii. 2
nice, unimportant, trivial. iii. 1; v. 2
note, set music to. iv. 5
O, lament. iii. 3
o'erperch, fly over. ii. 2
orb, concentric sphere which carries planets and stars with it in its revolution. ii. 2
outrage, fury. v. 3
overwhelm, overhang. v. 1
palmer, pilgrim from the Holy Land. i. 5
parlous, dreadful. i. 3
part, party, side. i. 1
partisan, a long-handled spear with a blade having lateral cutting projections. i. 1
passado, forward thrust with the sword, one foot advanced at the same time. ii. 4; iii. 1
passage, procedure. i. prol. 9
pastry, place where pastry is made. iv. 4
physic, medical faculty. ii. 3
pilcher, scabbard. iii. 1
pin, stud fixed in the centre of a target. ii. 4
point, point of the sword. iii. 1
poise, weigh, estimate. i. 2
poor-john, salted hake (a type of poor fare), i. 1
poperin, variety of pear; from Poperinghe, a town in West Flanders. ii. 1
portly, stately, dignified, majestic. i. 5
possess, seize, take possession of. iii. 2
post, post-horses. v. 1
presence, presence-chamber. v. 3
prick, remove by a prick. i. 4; minute-marks on a clock. ii. 4
prick-song, accompanying melody to a plainsong. ii. 4
princox, pert saucy boy. i. 5
private, alone. i. 1
procure, get a person to do something. ii. 2; bring. iii. 5
proof, tested strength of armour or arms. i. 1

prorogue, defer. ii. 2; iv. 1

punto reverso, back-handed thrust. ii. 4

reclaim, reduce to obedience, subdue. iv. 2

reeky, full of rank moisture. iv. 1

refuse, decline to hear. ii. 2

region, air, heaven. ii. 2

respective, partial. iii. 1

rest, repose. v. 3; may God give rest to, may God keep you. i. 2; &c.

ropery, trickery, knavery. ii. 4

roses, cake of, preparation of rose petals in the form of a cake, used as a perfume. v. 1

runagate, vagabond. iii. 5

rush, strewn on floor for reception of visitors. i. 4

rush aside, brush aside. iii. 3

sad, sadly, sadness, grave, gravely, seriousness. i. 1; &c.

safety, safe custody. v. 3

scant, scarcely. i. 2

season, give a spice, relish, or zest to. ii. 3

set, regard, esteem. v. 3

shield, forbid. iv. 1

shrift, confession and absolution. i. 1

shrive, hear confession and give absolution. ii. 4

sick, of a sickly hue, pale. ii. 2

simple, medicinal herb. v. 1

singleness, simplicity, silliness. ii. 4

single-soled, contemptible, mean. ii. 4

sirrah, familiar style of address. i. 5

skeins-mate, ? knavish companion. ii. 4

slip, counterfeit coin. ii. 4

slop, loose breeches. ii. 4

small, thin, fine. i. 4

smatter, chatter. iii. 5

soho, hunting-cry used when a hare was descried. ii. 4

solace, be happy, delight. iv. 5

soundpost, part of a violin, used as a musician's name. iv. 5

sphere, orbit of a planet, or of the eyes. ii. 2; &c.

spinner, long-legged spider. i. 4

stand on, stand upon, be particular about. ii. 3

stratagem, deed of great violence. iii. 5

swashing, ? dashing, swinging. i. 1

sweeting, sweet kind of apple. ii. 4

tackled stair, rope ladder. ii. 4

take me with you, let me understand you. iii. 5

tassel-gentle, tercel, male of the peregrine falcon. ii. 2

temper, modify. ii. chor. 14; compound. iii. 5

tetchy, fretful, peevish. i. 3

timeless, untimely, premature. v. 3

tithe-pig, pig paid as a tithe. i. 4

top-gallant, highest mast of a ship; hence, summit. ii. 4

toy, idle fancy, whim, freakish thought. iv. 1

trow, dare say. i. 3

truckle-bed, low bed, which could be pushed under another. ii. 1

unadvised, inconsiderate. ii. 2

unattainted, unbiased, i. 2

uneven, not straightforward. iv. 1

unmann'd (in falconry), not accustomed to the presence of man. iii. 2

unstuffed, untroubled. ii. 3

utter, offer for sale. v. 1

validity, value. iii. 3

vanish, escape from. iii. 3

vaulty, arched, cavernous. iii. v

versal, universal. ii. 4

visor, vizard, mask. i. 4

waggoner, charioteer. i. 4

wanton, trifler, i. 4; luxuriant. ii. 5

wax, man of, wax model. i. 3

whoreson, used in coarse playfulness = fellow. iv. 4

wild-goose chase, race between two horses, the rider who leads choosing the
course, which the other is bound to follow. ii. 4

wits, five, viz. common sense, imagination, fancy, estimation, memory. i. 4

womb, anything hollow. v. 1

world, life. iii. 1

worm, humorously supposed to infest the fingers of lazy persons. i. 4

wretch, used as a term of endearment. i. 3

ABOUT THE INTRODUCER

WILLIAM HAZLITT (1778–1830) was born in Maidstone, Kent, England. A prolific essayist, political journalist, lecturer, and literary critic, he was one of the most prominent critical historians of the nineteenth century. His essay on *Romeo and Juliet* was adapted from his book *The Round Table: A Collection of Essays on Literature, Men and Manners* (1817) for this Modern Library edition.

A NOTE ON THE TYPE

The principal text of this Modern Library edition
was set in a digitized version of Janson,
a typeface that dates from about 1690 and was cut by Nicholas Kis,
a Hungarian working in Amsterdam. The original matrices have
survived and are held by the Stempel foundry in Germany.
Hermann Zapf redesigned some of the weights and sizes for Stempel,
basing his revisions on the original design.